The Intimacy of Consciousness Exploration and Transpersonal Psychotherapy:

Coming Home

The Intimacy of Consciousness Exploration and Transpersonal Psychotherapy:

Coming Home

Edited by

Ingo B. Jahrsetz, Regina U. Hess, Judith Miller and Rainer Pervöltz

Cambridge Scholars Publishing

The Intimacy of Consciousness Exploration and Transpersonal Psychotherapy: Coming Home

Edited by Ingo B. Jahrsetz, Regina U. Hess, Judith Miller and Rainer Pervöltz

This book first published 2017. The present binding first published 2018.

Cambridge Scholars Publishing

Lady Stephenson Library, Newcastle upon Tyne, NE6 2PA, UK

British Library Cataloguing in Publication Data
A catalogue record for this book is available from the British Library

ISBN (10): 1-5275-0802-1
ISBN (13): 978-1-5275-0802-6

TABLE OF CONTENTS

Prologue

Rainer Pervöltz

Perhaps you have also had this experience: you wake up in the morning and feel lost. You search for the causes for your feelings and you might find a whole host of things. You can tell yourself that once again it happened; that you drank and ate too much the night before with your friends. Or snippets of memory begin to surface; there were those hazy dreams you had before the break of day, still in the darkness of the night, and you know that you woke up briefly, disturbed and without comprehension for the outlandish scenes that surely seemed not at all related to you...

Or it comes to your mind how often at this time of day, just after waking, you feel haunted by your troubles and sorrows, even by fears. And as always, you ponder and feel bemused, and try, here too, to find reasons why this is happening. The internal clock offers itself as an explanation, the naked crack of dawn, or the ugly thought that you could be more depressed than you try to delude yourself you are during the routine of your day. At a pinch, the sparsely entertained unlikelihood reemerges that your house may be located in an inauspicious energy field – damaging earth rays, imprudent architecture with regard to the cardinal points...

What remains – despite all your attempted explanations – is the feeling and the subjective fact that you seem to feel lost.

So what, you may say to yourself, at least you noticed. How many people are walking around and have lost themselves so basically that they don't even realize it anymore. It is such a great fear in the world, and so infinitely widespread are all the pain-provoking mechanical life-forms we adapted to as children. You can read about it everywhere. There is much lament about nothing being connected anymore; everything being specialized and cut off, scattered and particular; each individual living his or her separate life, alone and ultimately lonely.

Such thoughts – you notice – are not a good start, not any kind of basis on which to go into the new day with an appropriate amount of openness. They are gray and cloudy leftovers from the night, and what matters now is not to unduly feed this cloudiness but to pay attention to how to change it into a more bearable and fruitful attitude. Of course, you don't want to have to tell yourself that you made attempts to repress these uncomfortable early morning feelings, or even tinkered with the idea of simply tossing out the disturbing malaise. However, at this point, it might be good to stay in a certain remote aloofness and run through the habitual processes of your morning routines – which you anyway believe to be necessary to get you into a state of functional efficiency. Nothing advocates the conviction, as you secretly know, that after this routine (brushing your teeth, showering, eating breakfast, listening to the news) you will have returned to yourself. But you will have accepted the state of inner absence to such an extent that it won't make a difference anymore. You'll approach the challenges of your day now and will master them without any great difficulty.

A totally different perspective would appear if you were so shocked at the loss of your true being that before starting any of your daily automatisms, you used all means imaginable to find yourself again. Perhaps – you might hastily want to modify – this would presume a material framework you do not possess: a certain availability of time principally warranted by a reasonable money flow; no children screaming for security or lemonade; no colleagues waiting for you, no students, bosses or patients… At the same time, you may recognize that such pragmatic thoughts seem to be adequate and understandable but they might also be the best trick of your mind to prevent you from truly coming back to yourself.

As in all of us, there works in you an ancient and long-outdated system that you have learned and which specializes in protecting you from too much change and – more importantly – from your true being. It is infinitely pedantic in its attentions to make sure that you do not shine too brightly or for too long. It utilizes everything that promises that in the end, you get lost to yourself again.

One can't say that this system is evil. It only clings, based on your previous experiences, to the narrow perspective that it would be better to keep you away from yourself. It does not recognize nor accept the feeling of being profoundly and truly at home in yourself. The opposite, in fact; it considers this state to be risky and dangerous, and stubbornly refers again and again to those previous experiences in which you shone and received humiliation and rejection for it. So, it puts everything on the line to make sure these early pains will never be repeated.

Unfortunately, one cannot say that this old system is substantially led by intelligence. A kind of higher law seems to decree that any pain you are trying to avoid is especially unavoidable. An entity inside of you has assumed command and persistently drags this very pain back into the light and actualizes it – probably with the stubborn intent to spoil and embitter your addiction for avoidance to such an extent that eventually you will turn *towards* instead of *away from* it.

At the very least, it requires a great joy and a fiery passion that enable you to kindle deep inside your heart the desire to come home. At any rate, a strong inner turmoil is necessary because all that is mechanical, all that is repetitive, is made up of such stringent authority that every timid attempt to break free from the routine is suppressed before it can even germinate. This suppression doesn't need great efforts at persuasion. At every first opportunity, you yourself are all too happy to reactivate your, let's say, slightly whacky logic that helps you to stick to your conservative domestic policies. Whacky in the sense that, for years now, this logic has appeared reasonable to you, even though you still have not found your way home. And, unfortunately, you have to admit to yourself that this is why joy is seldom experienced, and much more often, feelings of great suffering wake you up and help you recognize your sad inner segregation. Why don't you understand these bleak morning hours as your souls cheerful, friendly attempts to go against the obstinate wackiness?

It is a fact, certainly regrettable, but you have to be *disturbed*. You need *disturbance* in your life so you can remember that you are not at home within yourself. Most of us are easy-going when there is nothing that annoys or irritates us. Quite often though, you have set off to look for what you seemed to have lost. You know this search and you have tried many ways to sense again in yourself the one thing you believe you have lost. And, as already mentioned, it is unfortunate but the search turns out to be more intensive and forward-pressing when you feel hopeless, desperate and helpless. A position of hopelessness, which disturbs and impedes your habitual life, brings you, if you allow it, closer to the consciousness of your inner separateness and can help you remember who you really are.

And what does this mean, what would you like to remember? Whatever you have learned to call it, it is always in some way or another the desire to "come home." This desire seems to spring forth from a strange and secret knowledge that somewhere in you there is a "place" where you are at home. At home – there is no pressure, no expectations, you can let go of everything, find yourself adorable and come to peace with life. There is this freedom of *not having to.* You sit when you want to sit and you get up when you want to get up. If you are able to enjoy home, you can live your entire potential and you don't have to. You also know –

or had more or less conscious experiences of it – that when you live your life from this place, everything is different. You've experienced it, you know it is possible: activity can arise from a state of release (instead of effort), the sympathetic from the parasympathetic, success from surrender. This place within us reminds us of the Great Dream-maker, who is also you, and of the creative intelligence that effortlessly opens up all paths when you manage to let yourself go.

To say "within us" is an incomplete form of our limited language. The linguistic deficiency results from the desire to be generally understood – and the general consensus calls for a differentiation between 'inside' and 'outside.' However, for some, what is within may be as easily found in the without; they may call it 'God' or 'Oneness' or 'dreaming' or 'non-locality.' Isn't it a shame that an arbitrary instruction to establish it here or there and call it such and such only turns out, again, to be a replication of the old system that keeps you apart from yourself. From a more distant perspective, it is painful to see how we prevent each other through petty righteousness and dogmatism from returning to where all of us truly want to be. It becomes even more bitter when this knowing-better attitude not "only" occurs out of a desire for power, as in the case of some religious institutes and their representatives, but stems from a compulsive desire to tell others how they should find their way home. More bitter because it simply isn't possible in the last consequence to lead others home. One could perhaps, on the basis of some elementary "geographic" knowledge, propose to another person a couple of key itineraries (go over the hill or go through the woods) yet only they alone can know in the end where their true home resides.

We are a team of psychotherapists and spiritual teachers who founded this training institute together and believe that good therapeutic teaching is based on good relationships. How we build relationships is in principle the same in all situations. Our relationships with our partners, friends and colleagues, our relationships to trees, to water and to God – are all marked by how close we are to ourselves, how good and how often we are at home within ourselves.

For this reason, some time ago, we acknowledged the fact that the kind of relationships we have among ourselves crucially influences the quality of our teaching. And so the idea arose to meet regularly in order to get to know each other better, with a particular focus on how far we can come home within ourselves and stay this way whilst engaging with each other.* It quickly turned out that the quality of our relationship with God (or the measure of being at home within ourselves) appears the clearest in situations where, despite all the difficulties, we have the courage to get closer.

In the middle of this risky undertaking came the idea that we could write a book about the whole thing. If each one of us could open up about our own and unique 'homecoming,' putting all of our stumbling blocks and curveballs into writing, then we could perhaps fashion something out of these texts that might result in a book. And at the same time, this project impacted our team in the way of a refined ability to relate.

You are holding the result in your hands. It was a great challenge for all of its contributors. Talking about God is something very intimate and continually took us to our limits whenever we weren't quite ready to surrender our privacy. And yet we are happy now that it was so difficult. We wish you great joy while reading this, and hope it presents you with countless inspirations on your own itinerary.

*In Judith Miller's Epilogue in this book, she writes more comprehensively about this subject.

INTRODUCTION

WHERE WE ARRIVE

TOM STEININGER

A group of psychotherapists and spiritual teachers write a book about homecomings. However, they are actually a group of friends who want to explore something together: What actually *is* "home"? In the process, they create sketches of personal quests, individual searches for a "home." And in these different ways, a book about God came about.

Where do we *actually* arrive at when we "arrive"? Where have we been in the meantime? For the authors of this book, this has been a recurring theme in their working lives. As psychotherapists and spiritual teachers, they have guided people on this path for many years.

Before we began this book, we held a private meeting with all the authors. In her contribution, Judith Miller describes how this meeting led to the creation of this book: "During this encounter, the same question kept popping up: how do we become closer and more open with one another – despite our many differences of nationality, gender, personal style and culture being deciding factors?"

And then Rainer asked, "Does everyone feel at home here in this group, in our institute?" I remember saying no. "Believing that I could really feel at home here would be unrealistic," I replied. "The institute is mainly made up of Germans, and you see each other regularly – but not me. Also, I'm a Jewish American woman, and there is still some mistrust buried inside me due to the German/Jewish narrative," I admitted. I felt moved and vulnerable as I said this.

For several moments there was silence. My eyes felt moist. *What am I doing here?* I thought. And then, suddenly, several voices piped up – some were combative, some were contrite, some were empathetic. I felt as if I had laid myself bare. But it was all okay. I had been heard. And this led us to a deeper level of communication than ever before.

We discussed the meaning of "homecoming." What does it mean to each of us to "come home"? Someone said that homecoming for him meant being with God. Others in the group agreed. Some were uncertain and thought the expression "God" shouldn't be used. An intense discussion ensued. We all expressed deep feelings about each of our very personal journeys home.

From this sprung the idea to write down these thoughts. Manuscripts were written. We sent them to each other. There was another meeting so we could work on some of these stories of homecoming as a group. Thus, a very personal book was created. Here are the stories of nine people and their journey home together.

Humans have a home. Or humans are searching for a home. All the cultures in the world have stories about this particular place that is so important to us. Since the dawn of languages, we have been asking for it. And, fundamentally, it is often a quest for God. In the myths of world cultures, this question can appear in many different shapes and forms.

China is the "Middle Kingdom." Even this self-description says a lot about the home of the Chinese. China's first emperor, the mythical founder of Chinese culture, the Yellow Emperor Huáng Dí, reigned on the world mountain *Kunlun*, from which he held together the earth and the sky, holding it in a harmony of above and below, with the middle containing human culture. Even today's Communist China acknowledges the traditions of this legendary emperor and his attempts to keep the word culture in harmony on his mountain.

India is a country of rivers and streams. The *Indus*, which lent the country its name (although it flows mostly through Pakistan), has determined the flow of the land for thousands of years, along with the holy *Ganges*. These mighty rivers in South Asia find their source in the area of *Mount Kailash* in the Himalayas, the mythological mountain *Meru,* seat of the gods and protectors, the center of the universe. The *Vedas* say that the sun and the moon, the stars and the planets that decide the order of night and day, the coming and going of seasons, and also the well-being of humanity all circle around it. Modern India still sees itself as a country of *Vedas* and the gods and the stars still circle around the mountain *Meru today.*

Europe also has its myths, its ancient gods and holy mountains. But Europe is different. Our myths are different. The gods of the Greek Olympus were already gods of revolt against the old. Zeus and his cohort drove out Chronos, the Father of Zeus, and so the ancient Titans were driven from their seat of power. But even the Greek gods were toppled. The God of the Christians pushed the old Olympian gods into the shadows of the past.

Yet even the Christian God has been displaced from the altars of Europe. The Jacobites placed statues of the goddess of rationality in the churches of revolutionary France. By the time of Nietzsche, the news had spread throughout Europe that the Christian God was dead – that we had killed him.

We have continually left our old home. Europe is a culture of awakenings. We are constantly treading into new spaces. Perhaps these constant movements were prophesized in our myths, in our expulsion from Paradise. It is a story that still has a deep effect on us today. Why did we taste from the Tree of Knowledge? Why did we have to leave?

In Greek mythology, there too were discoveries and awakenings. It wasn't just the Olympian gods who overcame the ancient gods of Chronos and Gaia. The Greek heroes are also heroes that emancipated themselves from their ties to the old gods. *Odysseus*, perhaps the first modern European, overcame the magical powers of the sorceress Circe through his bright, thinking mind. The sorceress with her bewitching voice could not seduce him to his downfall. Odysseus had planned ahead, and before his ship sailed passed Circe's island, he had ordered his men to plug their ears with wax. He had himself tied to the mast so he could hear the sorceresses' song without falling to his death.

Through *Odysseus,* we began to free ourselves of the might of the gods. But in doing so, we left our old home behind. The end of ancient times was also the end of a time the gods walked the earth. The new God was different.

A personal God. Church fathers such as St Augustine demonstrated how they could connect with God in a personal dialog. But St Augustine's God stood above the world. He was not a part of it. He left the world to us. As we left the Christian God behind with the dawn of modernity, we alone were left behind. The Greek cosmos had been a place of safety.

Through modernity, we discovered a new feeling of being lost. The philosopher *Blaise Pascal* described a new awareness of life at the beginning of the 17th century: Because what is the human in nature really? It is nothing in comparison to the infinite, which is everything compared to nothing, something between nothing and everything.

So what can he do but be aware of a glimmer in the midst of things of the perpetual hopelessness of the fact that he has neither a source nor a goal?' Since *Pascal*, the cosmos has become a place in which we feel less and less at home.

But we did not stop searching for this home. The German Romantics went in search of the blue flower. According to the philosopher *Hegel*, the world spirit loses itself in humanity in order to ultimately find a future in mankind. This is also expressed in the absurd writings of the existentialists who came to the fore in the 20th century, such as *Albert Camus*, who accompanied the absurd with a sense of longing. What did *Samuel Becket* call it? – Waiting for Godot.

The feeling of estrangement has become a part of us. And this feeling constantly spurns us to continue our search:

> I am searching for the blue flower,
> I search and yet I never find it,
> I dream that in this flower,
> My good fortune will bloom.
>
> Joseph von Eichendorff, 1975[1]

Ironically, it was *Blaise Pascal,* student of the great European thinker of Enlightenment *René Descartes*, who, upon his death, was found to have a piece of paper sewn into the lining of his coat. *Blaise Pascal's Memorial*, as it later became known, had the following text:

> The year of grace 1654, Monday, 23 November, feast of St. Clement, pope and martyr, and others in the martyrology. From about half past ten at night until about half past midnight, Fire. God of Abraham, God of Isaac, God of Jacob, not of the philosophers and of the learned. Certitude. Certitude. Feeling. Joy. Peace. God of Jesus Christ. I have departed from him, they have forsaken me, the fount of living water, My God, will you leave me? Let me not be separated from him forever.[2]

Even our most enlightened philosophers were often driven to search for a Home. This estrangement – feeling like a stranger in the world – has become a bigger theme in the 20th century. It has shaped workers' uprisings as well as romantic popular movements. The cultural catastrophes of the 20th century were catastrophes in search of a new or old home. The narrative of Europe is one of constant departures, and yet we are perhaps more driven than our forefathers and mothers in our search for a home. In the past decades, the psychotherapy movement and a new spirituality have become a part of this search.

My home is *Linz*, one of the bigger Austrian cities, directly on the River Donau. In the north is the picturesque Muehlviertel, which leads to the heights of the *Boehmer Forest. Adalbert Stifter* first captured this out-of-the-way, insular landscape 150 years ago in his novels.

---

[1] Joseph von Eichendorff, poem: *Die Blaue Blume* [The blue flower] Rasch, 1975.
[2] Romano Guardini, 1935/1966, On faith and reason in *Blaise Pascal's Memorial.*

The south offers a view across the foothills of the Alps, all the way to the peaks of the Austrian limestone Alps. My family home lies on a hill in the city, and on a clear day, you can see both of these views to the north and south.

One of the first paths that I was allowed to go on by myself as a child was the way down the mountain into town, to the kindergarten. Halfway down this path, what fascinated me was the great gate to the *Maerzenkeller*: big gates that led directly to the middle of the mountain. The *Maerzenkeller* was a big wine and beer cellar in the city. Only decades later would I learn that these gates were originally built to house an air raid shelter during the war. Back then, nobody told me that the cellar that I saw on my way to the kindergarten had been built by prisoners of war in the 1940s, that the *Maerzenkeller* in the middle of Linz was once an external camp to the *Mauthausen* concentration camp.

On this hill, there is a striking settlement of vast social housing for the workers and employees of the Austrian national railway. These houses became a part of my childhood. Their almost pastoral farm-like architecture, with their big shared gardens, shaped my idea of what home was.

The long laundry lines that dominated the gardens don't exist anymore but my memories of them is a constant reminder of my childhood. These big settlements were known to us children under one name, which at the time we used quite nonchalantly, not understanding the connotations. They were the *Hitlerbauten,* Hitler buildings that were constructed in Linz during the war to provide housing for the workers in the arms industry.

Near our house, a path led down the hill to the Linz train station, and then on to town. This path led from a suburb of Linz, the village of *Leonding*. Every morning, traffic would flow from Leonding to Linz. And in the evening, the commuters would flow back. A hundred years ago, most would have traveled this way on foot. One was a small boy who walked to school every day from Leonding to town – this student was *Adolf Hitler*. His journey passed almost direct by my childhood home. He probably took this path when he visited Linz's music theater at least once a week to see productions of his beloved Wagner operas. I knew none of this as a child, but it is still a part of what I recognize to be my childhood home.

Our church in Linz was different. Built in the 1960s, the church nave was made from modern concrete, and the thirty-meter-tall altar picture was my introduction to modern art. Back then, I enjoyed going to mass. This partly had to do with the difficult family circumstances at home. Every Sunday, when I would leave my parents and siblings in order to attend ten o'clock mass in God's modern house, there was something different between us. I couldn't put my finger on what it was, and it never lasted long, but because of this Other that I met in that modern church, it became to me a place of trust. Even today, whenever I visit a church, it is a kind of arrival. An arrival in my childhood but also an arrival in an unknown dimension that I met back then for the first time. These places would become very important to me.

One of these places was a mountain. The *Krippenstein* is located in the Austrian *Salzkammergut*. It was my first encounter with high mountains. Every year before Easter, my family would drive to the *Krippenstein* to spend a week there skiing. Since the 1950s, you could actually go up the *Krippenstein*. There, not far from its peak at a height of 2000 meters and amidst boulders, ice and snow, sat a mountain hotel. On a clear day, you could look all the way down in the *Trauntal* far below. Everything you could see from up there was part of the mountain range. If you floated in a cable car up the *Krippenstein* mountain, you could see a little peak just after a vast rock face, which I always looked forward to as a child. Once you had crossed over this little peak, the valley would suddenly disappear from below you. The river, the streets, the villages and the sometimes already green fields would disappear in an instant. Afterwards – the cable car would be far beyond the line of trees – there would be nothing but the white of the snow and the clouds, the rough gray rocks and, if the weather was good, a shining sun and a deep blue sky. In the distance, you could see the other peaks of the *Dachstein* mountain range, and in the middle was the glacier highland. Every time we went up in the cable car, we would leave our populated world behind and come to a place that lay somewhere between heaven and earth.

The first trip up the mountain to the hotel at the beginning of each season was always especially impressive; it was as if a curtain to another world, almost forgotten, was suddenly pulled aside and you remembered how much you really felt at home here. And then, for a whole week, this commute between two worlds would ensue: if you were good at skiing, you could manage at least ten trips down the high mountain into the valley. At the bottom was the road with the car park, the cars, and not far from there was the next village. Above it was the sky, rocks, ice and snow. If you went skiing down into the valley, there was this one bend in the path that would lead to a glimpse of the rivers and lakes below. And if you took the cable car upwards, there was this little peak. After that, there was just the lonely mountain range.

Daily, at about 5 pm, the last cable car would glide up to the hotel then would shut down for the night, and we, along with the small group of hotel guests, would be trapped at the top of the mountain – sometimes during snowstorms, sometimes in the mellow glow of the evening sun. The world "down there" had been locked away. For breakfast – just before the first cable car – my family would sit in the dining room by the big windows. In front of us, if the sun was out, we could see the glistening glacier landscape of the *Dachsteinmassiv*. Breakfast in the mountains. It was a view that would not leave me for the rest of my life.

Many years later, as an adult, I had an experience during a long meditation retreat that led me to better understand what these childhood experiences really meant to me. After days of deepest silence, I was moved to realize that I had discovered something inside me that I hadn't felt since my childhood in the mountains.

It is most likely our spiritual experiences that are the true homecoming yet *Ingo Jahrsetz* writes at the very beginning of his essay in this book: "My home – I was born in 1943, in Breslau/Silesia. My mother gave birth in the Breslau local hospital; she was terrified, and so were the nurses who helped her give birth. As I then spied the so-called 'light of day,' it was really just a lamp that gave of no more than a weak glow." In reading his words, I am getting to know him as a person. I suddenly grow very close to him.

I felt the same when I read the surprising words of *Regina Hess*: "At around 8:30 am, I heard my friend, who was running towards my hut at the beach, shouting: "Run, run, Regina!" When I stepped out of the hut, all I could see was a huge black wall of water. Within moments, the monstrous wave struck and was I tumbling under water." Regina was in Thailand in 2004 with her friend when the tsunami hit the Southeast Asian country. This moment, in which she was gripped by the black wave, opened a connection between us that I will never forget.

And when *Stefan Dressler* writes about failure as a form of homecoming, that too changed my understanding of what it means to arrive: "All of these moments of great failure (of breaking taboos, of accepting a part of me I had always rejected, struggling with my demons, the identification with the demon principle), which are necessary for a hero/heroine, are inner processes of death and rebirth. In these moments of death, I am showing my true vulnerability, I am accepting the risk, accepting the fear. In these moments, my stubbornness relents, gives up control. These moments are not simply mental decisions, they really do occur. They are moments of submission and of devotion."

Where do we arrive – even us modern Europeans – when we arrive home? This is a book about God. But it is also about a God that saw Breslau in 1943, a God that went to the Linz opera with a young *Hitler*, a

God that swept himself up into a gigantic tsunami, and an arrival that we can only experience through failure.

Our modern world is multi-faceted and complex. Where do we want to arrive when we arrive at home here? Arriving is always associated with a feeling of ease. This is more than a naïve desire. The ease of it shows that we have lost something. In this way, seemingly "simple" people become our teachers.

Last year, some Indian friends invited me to the mountains of the southern Himalayas. For over twenty years, they have been running a school project in the mountain villages north of the town *Mussoorie*, and this project has changed not only the villages but also my friends. Some of these villages still have no road access, and it was my friends who opened the first schools in the region. Thinking back to their first expectations when they began this project makes them laugh today.

Even though they managed to bring education to thousands of children, my friends mainly talk about how these villages and their inhabitants have become their teachers. These villages have been around for thousands of years. Until recent times, their isolated valleys were their entire world. Their lives were shaped by the rhythm of the seasons, by the morning rain, and the many festivals of the Indian gods, who are just at home in the valleys and mountain ridges as the humans and animals. Many gods of the *Mahabharata*, the old Indian epic, live in these mountains, just as they did thousands of years ago. Every morning at dawn, the bells ring and the daily morning chant can be heard in the tiny mountain temple. In this part of India, the fate of the traveler lies in the goodwill and the blessing of the gods. Odysseus has not yet arrived in these mountains, but *Brahman* is here. Most of the time, he dances in the form of Shiva through the forests. My friends, these no-longer young intellectuals from *Delhi* and *Mumbai*, have found something they call Home amongst these people in the mountains.

Where do we arrive when we come home? Is it in moments of deep spiritual experiences? The house of our parents? The snow of the mountains that lets us realize how beautiful the planet is that we call home?

The authors of this book tell their own stories, and yet it is also a communal narrative. We meet each other as readers and writers in the midst of this fragile and complex world.

Perhaps this is the true Homecoming – in the midst of life.

References

Guardini, R. (1935/1966). *Pascal for our time*. New York: Herder. pp. 33-44.

Rasch, W. (1975) (Ed.). *Joseph von Eichendorff. Sämtliche Dedicate [All poems]*. München: Deutscher Taschenbuch Verlag.

CHAPTER ONE

COMING HOME

INGO B. JAHRSETZ

Abstract: All human beings want to be happy. "To come home", "to be myself" – these words speak about this deep human desire. We long for an overcoming of suffering. How this can happen is the teaching of all spiritual traditions. To support people to be happy and filled with life is the central theme of modern psychotherapy. This chapter tells the personal story of the author's homecoming. For him it is less a path and more a process of discovery and revelation of the sacred throughout his life and in very different situations.

Keywords: Coming home, human desire, life, overcoming suffering, spiritual traditions

Coming Home

Coming home – these words describe something that is perfectly ordinary and yet at the same time it is one of our deepest desires. Many people are at home during the night but not during the day.

They go to work – does this mean that they are not at home when they are at work? Many look forward to coming home afterwards, but not all. Some are very lonely. Being at home and being lonely – somehow this does not fit together.

During the 80s and 90s, my life was in a great state of upheaval. There were many disagreements in our little suburban house in a city in northern Germany. Being at home on the weekend was much more stressful for me than my time spent at work during the week. I was at home during the weekends. But was I at home there?

Today, I am often at home whether I'm at work or not. My office and my apartment are in the same house. I travel a lot for work. I mostly give seminars through which I help other people to "come home." When I travel, I live in seminar houses. I also feel at home in them, even when I am away from my home. Today, I usually feel at home even if I am very far away from Freiburg, my hometown. I usually feel at home when I am traveling. Yet, when I travel back to Freiburg after a journey, I am still excited to return home.

What is it, this concept of "home"? It seems to be something entirely paradoxical, something that is easy enough to comprehend but still seems to defy our true understanding.

An experience of home is something that mystics, such as Master Eckhart, often talk about. God is always within us yet we are so seldom at home.

'God' is a difficult word for me because it can so easily be just another concept among the innumerable individual, cultural and collective concepts that make up our world.

I would like to posit that in many cases, the word 'God' is used in an inflated sense because most people are driven by a desire to finally arrive home. Desire can sometimes be closely bound to addiction. The idea of encountering God and coming home to him can be used to fill the same void that alcohol or other drugs try to fill.

There is a long history of confusion and misunderstanding about God that, even today, still fuels violent clashes. Always at its heart, however, is the most important aspect of human existence: a truth that does not allow for any ambiguity.

Even today, almost 200 years later, Ludwig Feuerbach's words can still cause outrage, that religion is "opium for the masses." Some (older) readers might remember October 4, 1957, the launch of the first satellite into space and the tremor of shock around the world (the Sputnik Shock). I vividly remember the ironic unsettling tone of the newscaster's voice as he said that the (then) Soviets had shown by their launch of Sputnik that there is no God in space but only the laws of nature. This took place during the Cold War and, of course, it had great political implications.

For the collective as well as the individual, when "God" no longer fills a void, when the religious drug has lost its power, we are left to confront our fear.

Fear is very basic. It is probably our modern expression of suffering, the first of the four Noble Truths with which Buddha's first teaching in Sarnath, the Wheel of Buddhism, began.

Stephen Batchelor (1986) discovered that the Pali word 'dukha' = 'suffering' must be regarded as an incorrect translation today. The mistake stems from Victorian times and reflects the beliefs of that time. A more apt translation today would be 'fear', which is at the core of every human life.

It is the fear of human vulnerability (illness), the fear of transience (aging) and the fear of the dissolution of the self (death). The fear of insanity – a taboo in modern psychotherapy.

My Home

I was born in 1943 in Breslau, Silesia. World War II was at its peak. The Final Solution for the Jews had been decided at the Wannsee Conference and the Scholl siblings were executed for their involvement in the White Rose[1] movement in 1942. At the Casablanca Conference in 1943, the Allies decided on an unconditional surrender from Germany and Japan. At a Nazi rally, Goebbels asked, "Do you want total war?" A frenetic "Yes" was the answer from the masses. Stalingrad and the hail of bombs that annihilated so many German cities occurred in 1943.

I was born in a hospital in Breslau; my mother was terrified and so were the midwives. As I greeted the so-called 'light of the world,' I saw just an old, worn lamp that was nothing more than a weak glow.

This memory came to me through a dramatic and emotionally suffocating experience of Holotropic Breathwork. After hours of a painful struggle between life and death, unexpectedly, life succeeded. I was born, but I did not know what I was doing in the world. Of course, I knew that I should be here but I felt completely unwelcome. Every man and every woman had better things to worry about than making a newborn feel welcome.

I knew that this city was not my home, that this world was not my home. And yet, I lived. I needed many decades to understand that life, even my life, is a miracle.

In January 1945, in temperatures of -20 degrees Celsius, the entire German population of Breslau was chaotically evacuated. People were allowed to take only what they could carry. A never-ending stream of evacuees formed. Occasionally, low-flying planes shot into the crowds.

At that time, I was about one-and-a-half years old. There are estimates that only 3% of the children survived. My mother loved me very much; this is the only explanation I have for the fact that I survived.

My mother and I, my grandmother and my grandfather fled together. We were overjoyed to eventually find a train that was heading west. We lived on this train for an entire year. It became our home. It provided

---

[1] The White Rose was a student resistance group that acted against the Nazis. In February 1943, while handing out flyers at the University of Munich, Hans and Sophie Scholl were discovered by a caretaker and betrayed to the Gestapo.

protection from the storms and the cold. I do not know how my grandfather continually managed to find us food. Our lives on the train were, however, constantly in danger; stationary trains were always targets for bomb strikes. But childhood cannot be put on hold. There were times when I endangered everyone by simply peeing or doing other things. I know that sometimes my mother must have wished I were dead even though she loved me deeply.

Sometimes, on clear nights, my mother dared to venture outside the train with me. We could briefly escape the tight confines and the (sometimes stinking) chaos of our home, go out into freedom and fresh air that could not be destroyed by the pestilence of the waging war. My mother held me in her arms and we gazed at the moon and the stars. Their clarity, their light, the sublime reaches of the sky were a comfort and a sign of hope for us. Moon, my mother later told me, was one of my first words. Then there were the silences that seemed infinite and deep.

I felt at home in those moments. The clearness of the sky with the light of the stars, its silence that was far more than the simple absence of noise, a silence that was undisturbed by words. There was something, an untouchable presence, beyond this daily hell.

Today, I would say that there was something the little boy back then felt, so full of reverence that to speak its name would be blasphemy. It was the God who manifested himself in the thorn bush, saying, "I am who I am."[2]

My mother and father tried very hard to build a new home for our family after the war. We eventually had a roof over our heads, and it was always comfortable and we always had enough to eat. My parents did everything possible for us children. In this way, they showed their love for us.

However, they were seldom 'in themselves' at home. How could we children then feel at home? I remember the first year after the war: depressed, harried people. We had every possible excuse to cry and scream, but there were no tears and we did not scream because we did not want to alert the neighbors. Back then, we lived in a small apartment with thin walls. Our family drama unfolded within them.

I always felt superfluous as a child. Once, I ran away from home when I was five. I wanted nothing more than to die yet the berries I ate were not poisonous. When I returned home, no one had noticed that I had run away.

It is said that the family is a steadfast fort, a home, a castle that defends you from all the evil in the world. My family life was full of expectations,

[2] The Bible. Ex 3.2

full of abuse and domestic violence. There was a thick blanket of silence over everything. There was a great lie that I only noticed when I began to lie constantly. I condemned myself into a hell of lies from which there was no escape.

Even today, after many new so-called corrective experiences, I am still skeptical of family life. My experience of family was connected to the war, the struggle for survival and a deep sense of discomfort. My mother and father wanted us to have a home as a family but I did not feel at home. It was not until much later that it became clear to me that this actually was my home.

What is 'Home'?

This is the affair with God.

The city in which we lived after the war had many old churches. Almost all of them had been hit by bombs during the war. To me, as a little boy, it appeared as if God had been destroyed. In one of these churches, the *Marienkirche*, an emergency mass took place on Sundays, in one of its undamaged sections. The whole thing was always pretty creepy: those grey-clad scared people searching for comfort in a ruin. The broken and fire-damaged bells of St. Mary lay next to the seats in the congregation.

Mass was held by different priests. I remember that one of them would scream horribly throughout his sermons (probably in the misguided attempt to rattle our paralyzed hearts). With every scream, a shock of fear would pass through my body. I was afraid to go into the church, I was afraid of the priest, whom I believed stood next to God. I always prayed that he would not scream that day.

God was almighty in his mysterious way. I was afraid of God. It was an even greater fear than my fear of being beaten by my father whenever I came home too late.

What kind of God wanted to scare me with his screams? What kind of omniscient God was he? My parents told me he could see everything: all my small sins, which I believed could grow into criminal deeds, like the bombs that exploded his churches and his cities? Then there was the silence over the crimes, the mass murder that God did not want to see, that the little boy, however, had absorbed into himself.

This God was my constant companion. Did he have anything to do with my home, was he perhaps even my home?

When I heard the stories of people who were supposedly believers, and for whom the only salvation was God, I was uncomprehending, and only saw lies upon more lies. Today, I believe that faith in God is just another part of the great lie that enveloped everything back then, and which we almost allowed ourselves to merge into.

This lie separates us from our home, from those we love and from ourselves. The stories of God make the lies more believable. God himself had nothing to do with home.

What always drew me in were the moon and the stars at night. As a boy, I sought many paths to come closer to them. We lived in a city in which it often rained. I was often at a loss when I couldn't see the stars in the sky. Then there was the absoluteness of my father's gaze, who had lost himself in the struggle to rebuild everything that had been destroyed, and who aspired to kill my desire for the stars.

My Home is Dead

Wanting something and not wanting something replaced my desire for the open sky. For many years, I felt gripped by greed. I was under the spell of wanting or not wanting. It was the addiction to wanting to possess a home. It is common in my generation for this kind of greed to result in a prim terraced house and a suburban front garden.

The intensity of my greed saved me from losing my way. I wanted to own everything, every kind of material possession, but also a lot of things that were abstract, of the soul: a woman with perfect curves and an understanding and forgiving soul, constant sex and never-ending ecstasy, a job that didn't require effort or cause stress.

I wanted to own all those things but not the things that life offered me. It took a long time before I realized that the things I wanted could never become my home.

Even certain experiences of psychotherapeutic self-exploration, or psychedelic experiences, can bind us to this need to have and to own, even though they might seem to be enlightening at first.

I had many experiences of God. I thought I finally had 'it.' Of course, I did not.

I traveled many false paths to find my home. Sometimes it was very painful to find I had lost my way again. This always happened when I came close to fulfillment, when I had almost attained a desire. Something would always occur to show me that it was not what I wanted.

The question remains unanswered: where is my true home? Surely, it does not lie in the state of constant wanting or not wanting.

I find it very easy to understand why the Germans gravitated towards this state of wanting after the fall of the Nazi societal structures. In 1945, most of Germany's cities were nothing but ash and rubble. People wandered about without roofs over their heads or food to sustain them.

Families were torn apart. There were lost children without parents. Criminal gangs formed amongst the ruins, all in search of something to own. The dead lay everywhere. It was a time of uncertainty; was killing heroic or was it simply criminal?

Who should live, who should die? Cain, where is your brother Abel?

There was still this never-ending hatred for our Jewish brothers and sisters; the entire world hated the Germans. The Germans hated themselves and they took their vengeance out on each other. Personal quarrels were quickly settled with weapons. The war was not over after the War. History books make no mention of the dramatic increase in German suicides before and after the war. There were villages where 75% of the inhabitants committed suicide or had their friends kill them.[3]

'Heroic' feelings of guilt and shame suffocated people. It was a nightmare, a paranoid reality built on fear. The question of home mutated into a delusion of reality that ignored all answers. Was it a dream that pretended to be reality? Surely it must have been a nightmare of collective insanity.

God was broken. It was the end of the Christian Occident.

My life story made all this very clear to me. What we now experience collectively are mere attempts to emotionally and religiously repair things. We are trying to make this thing with God work again.

"Homecoming" - Marijuana

Death has always felt familiar to me; for many years, my life was overcast by a deep desire for it. In times of crisis, I contemplated bringing about my own death. The torturous possibility of killing myself followed me like a dark shadow for most of my young adult life. It reached its peak and almost became a done deal after the breakup of my first romantic relationship, which caused me extreme suffering.

Then there was marijuana. My friends surprised me with an invitation to smoke a joint with them one evening. I believed I had nothing left to lose, and I accepted.

It was a beautiful summer evening by a lake. We laughed together and felt connected. My heart opened and I felt an infinitely great love for my friends, the world and for myself. I felt that I had arrived home –

---

[3] David R. Beisel: Der deutsche Suizid von 1945 [The German suicide of 1945]. PDF in the Internet (undated).

surrounded by my friends and their unconditional zest for life, I felt my own heart open to cosmic love.

The spell of death had been broken, and my decision to kill myself was cast away and I never looked back. I never once toyed with the possibility of suicide again.

I understood something that evening: beneath my dance with death lay a dream, a bottomless desire for an endlessly deep relief full of peace and infinite quiet. I had rediscovered an opening in the sky that I remembered so vividly from my childhood in the yearlong home we had found on the train, deep amongst the terror of flight, and the hell of the war. Something inside me that I didn't quite recognize understood what home meant. I knew it even though I did not really understand it. I knew what it was not, and I knew what direction I should look in order to find it.

What is the Deal with Death?

I continually felt that death itself could not provide comfort. My experience of my environment showed me it was usually inadvertent, a destruction, a grisly ending to something that was not ready to end.

It was only in people who had found a sense of peace before they were dying that I could see their calm acceptance of their time to die.

Death is a sharp cut through life. When it calls us, we have nothing else to wish for or to expect. I first heard this phrase at the Esalen Institute from Sogyal Rinpoche, a Tibetan master who spent his entire life exploring the Tibetan understanding of life and death.

Back then, I was disappointed by Sogyal's words; I had expected to hear exciting stories about his, and (perhaps) my, past lives. I wanted to be comforted and cosseted with the truth regarding human death. I wanted to hear that it's not that bad after all. I hoped he would say that when this life ends, you would get a new one, perhaps in a form that fit my former visions of grandeur and happiness. He did not say anything like that. I remember a particular sentence he said: "When death comes, we have nothing more to expect and nothing more to wish for."

I know that I am not alone in my fantasies and experiences of past lives. They belong to the postmodern dogma, which cannot accept the following concept: It is over, irretrievably over. Over. But this concept is exactly what we must deal with when we talk about death. It is the only way we can fully come to terms with it.

Can We Accept Death?

'Acceptance' is a word that provokes a lot of resistance and other hostile reactions, especially in our culture. One part of the humanist school of psychotherapy, for example, is critical of transpersonal psychology, saying that acceptance promotes anything from authoritarian personality structures to brainwashing. Psychotherapy is more about dealing with aspects of life in an emancipating way instead of simply accepting them (Daecke, 2010).

Transpersonal psychology is not entirely opposed to this but there may still be misunderstanding. Accepting aspects of your life, perhaps even delving into them, has nothing to do with submitting yourself to authoritarian structures, and nor is it a depressive strategy for avoiding conflict. Acceptance means no more than trusting your own perception: to see, to taste, to feel how other people and the world appear to be in this moment. What is often forgotten is the idea that acceptance is about the individual person and his or her reactions to the world, thoughts, feelings and concepts. Acceptance is also about accepting personal, individual and collective history.

Acceptance is linked to mindfulness. This is a meditative attitude, a broad, non-judgmental attentiveness, which binds together the perceiver and the perceived. The perceiver and the perceived recognize each other as pieces floating together in the stream of life.

This attitude is created through an attentive and conscious perception. Meditation gives us the opportunity to realize how lost we are in our dreams of wanting and not wanting.

For me, meditation is a part of my life; it is a certain kind of attitude towards aspects of life.

We can change our lives through mindful perception. We thereby can become conscious of who we are not: we are not our greed, aversion or ignorance, we are not our fears or the great terror; we are not the many concepts that try to secure these negative things.

All of this is means to "accept" things the way they are. Above all, in this way, we can recognize when we are not at home.

What Does Accepting Death Mean?

A question often put to me is whether we can accept death. I do not believe that we can. We can only accept dying. Meditation can prepare us for dying. The same is true for intimate relationships. They fail when they primarily focus on wanting or not wanting. Wanting to own love is one of the most painful ways in which death is denied. Every new phase of life, every existential decision, is about accepting dying. Writing a book is an exercise in accepting dying. This is the reason for writer's block. We have a limited self-determination over what we write; it is more of an insertion into a process in which the writing simply happens and which dissolves the desire for self-determination. I continually experience that I have no self-determination if I do not understand myself. Such self-determination, then, is impossible as long as I concentrate on what I want or do not want to own.

Such challenges are what many moments in everyday life are about. One of the main aims of modern psychology is to support people in finding their place in the framework of relationships so that they can find their boundaries and say "yes" and "no", to have the strength to focus on what they need.

All of this has to do with the strong self. A strong self enables us to be self-assured and gives us courage and confidence. It is anchored to our body and trusts its own instincts; a strong self decides what kind of people it wants to be with and in what ways. Having a strong self is incredibly worthwhile. With a strong self as a basis, you can solve many neurotic problems. Stress is transformed into relaxation and satisfaction. A strong self means a mature adult.

Can a Strong Self be a Home?

I have never had a strong self. The circumstances of my upbringing were unsuitable for this development. Instead, I took on the paradoxical strengths of life and death. Through all the adversity and familial entanglements, I (mostly) was aware of my mother's and my father's love, and I felt how much my parents also loved my siblings. Did I love my parents? I think only barely.

What was clear for me was that I deeply felt the never-ending silence, the clear starry sky that was untouched by the chaos of my childhood; its breadth and its light, the unconditional peace that radiated from that sky. All of it illuminated us: my parents, my ancestors, and even the little boy I used to be. We were all raised in the light of the stars; we were comforted by an infinite empathy, lifted and protected by the silence.

I sought my first therapist when I was a young man going through a difficult crisis. During one of our first meetings, he surprised me by alluding to the cosmic without knowing my deep connection to it. "You are a cosmic person," he said. It struck me like a lightning bolt in my then radical Marxist existence.

Today I realize that it was only because of that sentence (which probably came to him intuitively) that I let myself engage in therapy. Back then, I had a very strong distrust of the world and all its inhabitants.

In the following years, I learned a lot about the qualities of the strong self through different psychotherapeutic modalities. I am very grateful because they helped me overcome many inner and outer difficulties in my life, and provided a certain sense of order and responsibility.

However, I was never fully convinced that this self was truly me. I regarded it more as a constructed (though still useful) self, as a kind of crutch (that came with all the pros and cons of such a device) in all the different areas of my life.

I never took this self very seriously. Somehow I knew that I could find the deepest fulfillment in life without it.

Even when I participated in psychoanalytic therapy in later years, I was constantly asked, "What is it that you want?" I knew even then that my constructed strong self was not what was important to me.

For many years, I was torn between intuitive knowledge of the cosmic qualities of humanity and the chaotic cognitive and emotional patterns that always threw me into difficulties. I suffered and caused enormous pain and sorrow over and over again because of my neurotic personality structure that hardly could be subdued. Moreover, I tormented myself and others by trying to live a so-called normal life in the light of cosmic love.

Sometimes I constructed circumstances in my life, or sometimes I did it in different therapeutic or psycho-spiritual ways: I was destined to die a double death, the first because there was too little of the 'I'; the other because the 'I' was a hindrance to my surrender to the light of the universe, the void, ecstatic joy and love.

Annica, *dukha* and *an-atta* are Pali words in Buddha's language. *Annica* means everything that exists will be born and will die; everything that exists is subjected to a state of permanent flux. *Dukha* is the suffering and the fear that stem from the resistance to accepting changes. *An-atta* is the notion of the 'not-self' – it is the consciousness of our cosmic quality. We humans are stardust which, under certain circumstances, evolves into language and the ability for self-reflection, and each single individual realizes that it is evolution itself – new and unique.

My life is a process of an ongoing acknowledgment of dying. If I recognize suffering and the great fear, then I also recognize dying.

The most painful part of this has been the realization that my first home was the fascist war in Germany, in which my family had been embedded. Acknowledging this made it possible for me to honor and love my mother and father. In this way, I could see this country as my homeland.

I slowly learned to trust the light that would connect me to others through love.

I never expected to be able to come home in my city. But when I visited Breslau several years ago, I felt once more the memories of my childhood and my home, a destroyed city in the middle of the war.

"Homecoming" – A Popular Word in Obituaries

Death is not a home. It happens beyond us. When we are dead, there is nothing more to accept. But where am I when I am dead? When I am dead, who am I?

The Western scientific mainstream considers death to be the cessation of all brain functions. When the human body dies, there is nothing left. It is finality.

The postmodern worldview totally avoids this point. Even many in the psycho-spiritual movement turn away. Instead, the experiences that are looked at and discussed come from other cultural traditions in which rebirth is commonly accepted. It accepts accounts of near-death experiences, and of a spiritual rebirth in other dimensions. Representations of paradise in different cultures are often quite earthly and based on the desires and ideals of these traditions.

Is Paradise as a place a kind of 'great homecoming'?

It may seem like this to many people, and it gives them hope in their darkest hours. Such a comfort can be very helpful because the difficulties in our lives can easily become traumatic, paralyze our personality and close our hearts. Sometimes we need some solace that may transcend the truth and reality. It is like a mother holding her child in her arms and comforting it while both are in grave danger. It is often asked in psychotherapy, which came first: love or the truth? I would like to side with the first, even though I know that there are situations in human contact when it may be the other way around.

I do not believe in paradise as a place of homecoming. I personally gain nothing from this kind of belief. Death comes, it is the irrevocable end; and yet there is hope.

From where do I gain this certainty?

The problem with death is that we cannot experience it for more than a few minutes. Near-death experiences only occur for a few short moments.

Nobody has ever come back from the long-term experience of true death. As the story goes, Jesus was resurrected from death; this must be a legend that tries to intimate something that is difficult to understand.

Perinatal Experiences in Holotropic Consciousness

In holotropic consciousness, it is possible to have authentic experiences of dying, death and rebirth. I have personal experiences of these and have witnessed them during my therapeutic supervisions of others. These experiences can vary greatly and are in the realm of the perinatal, as Stan Grof (1985) refers to the archetypal region of consciousness around birth (Jahrsetz, 1999).

Perinatal experiences are of great value in terms of letting you learn more about yourself and your capacity to self- heal. Their actuality and therapeutic importance are barely acknowledged in mainstream psychotherapy, and they are even undervalued in transpersonal psychotherapy. When perinatal levels of consciousness are incorporated into therapeutic practice, perinatal experiences can transform the nature of psychotherapy itself. Psychology is a field that focuses primarily on strengthening the self, on achieving confidence, and on establishing boundaries. This is not enough.

By acknowledging and working with perinatal levels of consciousness, psychotherapy could support and guide people into an initiation, similar to the path of shamans and the mystery cultures. Holotropic states of consciousness have continued to demonstrate a high therapeutic efficiency when integrated in a therapeutic relationship.

An important aspect of perinatal experiences is the so-called 'ego-death', a term coined by Stan Grof (1985). In my opinion, this is a double-edged term because it can easily be confused with the dissolution of the self, as it is often described in old spiritual traditions. Those who have been through the ego-death in holotropic consciousness have experienced dying, death and spiritual release. But this is generally not a lasting experience. Everyone can have such an experience but afterwards (in the consciousness of everyday life) it can be interpreted in the context of the level of development (Cohen, A. & Wilber, K. 2006) the person presently is at.[4]

The perinatal ego-death is important as a clinical term. It is an authentic experience of dying, death and birth, which opens the gate into the transcendent. This kind of experience is all-encompassing. It encompasses

[4] See: Dialogue between Andrew Cohen and Ken Wilber (2006). See reference list.

the body, emotional expressions, thoughts and intuitive and spiritual understanding. In these states, people can have access to the individual as well as the collective knowledge of the world and, furthermore, to its many archetypes, to the consciousness of animals and plants, to the experiences of mystics. Experiences of holotropic consciousness are not an end in themselves. If they occur in a protected and safe context, they can bring about a deep healing of painful wounds.

In the present psycho-spiritual and "transformation" culture, the character of initiation is flattened and its core, the so-called ego-death or – as the shamans call it – the trinity of dismemberment, death and rebirth is avoided.

Is There Life Before Death?

I once read the phrase: "Is there life before death?"

The answer: yes, but what is life before death?

Usually the word 'life' brings to mind something that is vibrant and valuable, a happy life: having fun together, wealth, a fulfilled sexuality, a relationship full of lasting understanding that can be a stronghold against loneliness, a life without fear. Conflicts are rarely mentioned in this context, and you seldom hear the importance of creatively developing yourself in the world. Sickness, aging and death are never mentioned in the context of a fulfilled life.

According to the legend of Buddha, however, this is the most essential and existential fact of human life.

I experienced something entirely paradoxical: if we begin to plan and hope for luck and happiness to arrive home, we will instead come home to sickness, aging and death. This recognition was the basis for Buddha's teachings on how to overcome suffering. Buddha awoke in the starlight in the richness of the living world. He 'came home' in the night, under the fig tree.

Homecoming is dependent on whether we acknowledge death in ourselves. Die before you die so you may live is a saying of the great masters of the world.

This does not sound very optimistic, more like letting yourself be dragged down by the shadows of the world, cowering on the edge of an abyss of depression.

But this is not true.

Dying before death doesn't mean fighting your own vitality, perhaps feeling like a sinner, abasing yourself with humbleness as the Christian Church has preached.

Dying before death (or as some have called it, the dying of the ego, the ego-death) means daring to live genuinely. It may feel like the death of the ego leads to a greater inner wisdom. This wisdom comes when we have the same great courage that is required when we face dying. Dying before death also means that we may accept death in its many forms without discrimination, whether it's love or sorrow, and accept it as a gift.

Many people find it more challenging to accept joy, its power and the more positive side of life. Perhaps they know that real happiness isn't possible if they don't also face the smaller fears and the great fear.

I often meet people in very difficult situations, such as the loss of a job, the loss of a loved one, separations and death. Naturally, they fight the pain at first. Some of them first have to learn to stand up for themselves, to take responsibility for their circumstances.

Every animal defends itself against pain and is instinctively afraid of dying; humans don't want to feel pain either, and they try to ward off fears: they defend themselves against the fear of going insane, and the fear of death.

Personally, I found that the more I tried to fight it, the more I found myself tied up in intensively painful situations. In difficult times, I tried to distract myself in various ways by seeking out dangerous adventures. Even therapeutic work that tried to make me see that I didn't need the old patterns in my life led to no success. Instead, the opposite happened: the more I tried all these things, the more divorced I felt from myself, the less I felt at home anywhere in the world. The great pain was always there.

Eventually, I was completely exhausted and I gave up. I admitted that this terrible pain was a part of my life. In the depths of my pain, I admitted that I had no chance of making it disappear, or that I didn't even want to make it go away.

It all felt like I was dying. But this was the paradoxical moment, the point at which things turned for the better. And as a kind of a side effect, I felt more and more at home.

Homecoming, the Spiritual Path and the Psychological

Today, I no longer believe that there is a spiritual path. Meditation, singing mantras and other spiritual practices are no holier than doing the dishes or driving a car.

The belief in a spiritual path lies in a misunderstanding that the good, the true and the beautiful may be found one day in the most mysterious circumstances. It is a misconception that holy experiences and the gifts of heaven must be integrated into my life – as if the light of the stars can fit into the décor of my living room.

The mystery of life does not fit into your home. It is not the struggle over mine and yours, I want this and that by all means.

Greed and envy can transform into caring for yourself and gratefulness, and the universal drive to want things can change into something very unimportant. The house falls silent when borders are created. An aversion to wanting is formed and can be transformed into a trust in wisdom and the processes of life.

Knowing that it is not all about us, we can turn to ourselves. We then become still, connected by empathy.

The secret lies in our perception, in our discovery that we are always at home. This does require a lot of psycho-emotional work.

Ken Wilber (2014) once spoke about the fourth turning of the Buddhist wheel.[5] By that, he meant to recognize modern psychological knowledge, developmental psychology and neurobiology. I agree with this, yet I think that this is not everything by a long shot.

Even the integration of emotional therapeutic work into the *Dharma* (the wholeness and truth of Buddhist teaching) does not give us the certainty of having come home. From the perspective of psychotherapy, I would like to include the experiences of holotropic consciousness and the handling of normal life as well as the knowledge of psychological transference, which the grandmaster of transpersonal psychology, Charles Tart, called the greatest gift from the West to the East.

It is important that the spiritual traditions of the East and West move ever closer together. There are challenges in doing this, however. Joseph Campbell (1959) described the eastern Vedic understanding of the Atman as the sun, which is orbited by human beings. The more unimportant, the smaller these 'egos' are, the brighter the sun can shine. Such an understanding is often encountered today in the psycho-spiritual subculture of the West. Sometimes, however, because of the diminishment of psychotherapy, the clarification of emotional structures and other conceptual entanglements fall deeply into disrepute.

---

[5] The first turn occurred during Buddha's first lecture in Sarnath with the Theravada, the second in the Mahayana with the idea that the release was not just to be understood by individuals, but happened for the wellbeing of everyone, the insight of the Bodhisattwas. The third turn is about the 'Buddha-nature', which stands for the inner highest potential of human beings. Above all, it is the Tibetan Vajrayana, the inner understanding that all living beings can turn to Buddha. Wilber's suggested 'fourth turning' is about including modern psychological knowledge. See also: Michael Kauschke in Evolve, Synergia Verlag Rossdorf, 2014.

I think we are mistaken here. Especially after the wars of the 20th century, when the traditional values of the so-called Judeo-Christian Occident began to fall apart or at least become more brittle, we hardly ever find 'wholesome' family structures in western countries. Currently, I can observe a great confusion about what is actually understood as a homecoming.

What about the 'exterior house'? How much can our family, friendships and close relationships be a home? Do erotic relationships help us come home? Relationships between men and women? What is the masculine really, and what is the feminine? What does arriving within you mean? Is it about the integration of the inner child? Is it about taking responsibility for your own life? Is it about being an adult?

What is God in a thoroughly secular world? Is God a niche product? What is enlightenment? What do we mean by spiritual freedom?

Can we agree with Ken Wilber (2014) when he talks about the fourth turning of the wheel? This could also mean that spiritual release is possible without any emotional work.

Meditation as the Gift of Life

Meditating does not mean sitting and doing nothing. It is not as easy as you would think because most people in the West are focused on always doing things. Meditation means being 'lazy' and being aware of this.

When we sit still and do not move while meditating, it allows us to accept the gifts of life, the pleasant ones as well as the difficult ones. Meditation gives us attention and a consciousness for that which truly is. I agree with Martine Batchelor (1996) when she says that meditation is not about reaching an exotic experience of consciousness, nor is it about absolute breath control or completely emptying your mind of all thoughts. It is about being *conscious* of everything that is, the inner and the outer, and the *exploration* of everything that is, the inner and the outer.

I have practiced Vipassana meditation for almost 30 years and have discovered that it has become a part of my attitude towards life. My daily life now is not a romantic kind of living spirituality, with all its peace and nobility that I had hoped it would be. My life is still full of conflicts and unresolved issues, and there are also a lot of pleasant things that are creative and good.

Slowly, along the way, completely unexpectedly, a silence began to spread before me; it has no beginning and no end.

It is the silence that I experienced as a young boy in the nights on the train, at the end of the war in the cosmic silence, in which there was nothing but infinite love.

Now

It is the year 2017. We are in May.

There are many predictions for this year. Some talk about an uncomplicated, good year; others say that we are in the middle of World War III and Armageddon has begun.

I observed the unsettling escalation of the crisis in the Ukraine, in which for the first time in decades, the Eastern and Western powers are at a political and military standoff. The Ukraine is one of the poorest countries in Europe and the loser in a global economic competition. There are the continued murders in Syria, in the south of Sudan. Israel and Palestine have not reached peace, one of the many lasting consequences of the Holocaust.

Climate changes on earth have become something normal for many. In the past months, there have been natural catastrophes, floods of unforeseen vastness, an unusually harsh winter in North America and a much-too-warm winter in central Europe. Reports of the melting ice caps are openly accepted.

As I write this, I am sitting in a warm room on the outskirts of Freiburg. It is a little bit rainy today but when I look out of the window, I see the glory of the ever-blooming trees. I love my wife, though we have very different personalities that may sometimes clash in a conflict. I am grateful that my life incorporates a circle of near and close friends. I am grateful for the therapeutic and spiritual work I do with people who trust me.

This year, I have discovered that the people of Israel are brothers and sisters to us Germans. I am filled with guilt at being alive while millions of Jewish people were murdered by Germans. In Germany, there is still resistance to the belief that there was not simply a small clique of evil Nazis who seduced the great mass of good Germans, but it is like the tale of Red Riding Hood and the Wolf in which we all had our part to play.

My Life is My Message

My life has shown me how essential it is to take responsibility for yourself. It is nobody else's fault when I am unhappy; and there are no circumstances that are responsible for my well-being. I know that circumstances can sometimes be painful; I don't wish to be cynical. Yet in every death lies the chance for a new beginning and the realization of the clear light of truth. This light is the great secret, which we can only slowly, gradually approach with great reverence. We cannot understand this light yet we can understand its existence as a single 'I am.'

My life began in the middle of the most horrible time of the war; it began as my mother bore me and my body *wanted to* die. And yet it did not. I am on a never-ending journey, without time. It never began and it will never end.

My existence is a discovery: the comfortable as well as the uncomfortable, the shadows of the world, hunger, war and destruction. A fresh morning in the spring, flower pollen, the smile of the person you love. Light and shadow caught in love.

This is the stillness that is always present. Stillness that encompasses and contains everything. At first you may sense it in the space between amidst inhaling and exhaling. Or early in the morning between waking and the start of the day.

Stillness.

Clear starlight, the moon in the night and the sun in the day. We are creatures made of stardust, bound into a great net of light. Humans and all living beings are held and shine in the same way; everything affects everything else. For the last few months, an African word about the attitude to life has been on my mind: *Ubuntu* – I am because you are. And then there is the word that, if said out loud, becomes a curse.

Stillness – the act of dying before death.

Homecoming.

References

Batchelor, S. (1986). (Ed.). *The jewel in the lotus: A guide to the Buddhist traditions of Tibet*. Boston, MA: Wisdom Publications.

Batchelor, M. (1996). *Meditation for life*. Boston: Wisdom Publications.

Campbell, J. (1959). *The masks of God: Oriental mythology*. New York: The Viking Press.

Cohen, A. & Wilber, K. (2006). The evolution of enlightenment. The guru and the pandit. Ken Wilber and Andrew Cohen in dialogue. *What is Enlightenment Magazine Online*. Retrieved on April 30, 2017 from http://www.integralesforum.org/

Daecke, K. (2010). Über das Emanzipatorische in der Gestalttherapie - mit kritischem Blick auf deren spirituelle Wende [Emancipatory aspects of

Gestalt therapy - with a critical look on its shift to spirituality]. Lecture on the occasion of the congress "Gestalttage 2010." Vienna 2010.

Grof, S. (1985). *Beyond the brain: Birth, death, and transcendence*. New York: State University of New York Press.

Jahrsetz, I. (1999). *Holotropes Atmen, Psychotherapie und Spiritualität* [Holotropic breathwork, psychotherapy and spirituality]. Stuttgart: Klett.

Wilber, K. (2014). *The fourth turning: Imaging the evolution of an integral Buddhism*. Boston & London: Shambala Publications.

CHAPTER TWO

ALL WATER HEADS TOWARDS THE SEA

JAYA HERBST

Abstract: It is an undeniable fact that *change and movement* characterize the expression of life. The crucial question for us is: Do we accept the challenge of change and movement or do we fight it? We fear change because we are afraid of losing control over our life. It's only by becoming aware of our Divine nature that we can gain trust in life and the changes it inevitably brings to us. Becoming able to perceive and communicate with our expanded I-consciousness requires intensive training, which is worthwhile because it always creates a growth in love. And it is also worthwhile because it helps us gain confidence that we will pass safe and sound through all the turmoil and complications of life – and with that certainty, there is a power, which protects and upholds us.

Keywords: challenge of change, dynamics of motion, freedom of choice, energy, Higher Self consciousness.

Introduction

In my chapter, I would like to deal with how we can learn to trust our flow of life and acquire a positive attitude to the changes that are inevitable in order to progress. This trust only develops if we can establish contact with our divine plane of consciousness. Only then can it serve as an active trustworthy power that helps us shape our lives and make necessary decisions.

Coming home. How do we know where home is? How do we know what it feels like to be home? Maybe because we are like rivers. It is in the nature of a river to flow back to the sea and become part of it.

The idea of writing about spiritual processes in connection with psychotherapeutic work seemed to be quite simple at first but the intense discussions among the members of our team have shown me that it is only easy for me as long as I do not involve my personal experiences.

After deciding to do this in one part of the article, it became more difficult for me to explain these personal experiences and my inner attitude to them in words. First of all, I was worried that it might seem presumptuous to write about something I was perhaps not entitled to write about. But it felt also difficult to reveal something about myself that might make me vulnerable. To reveal something about me that is *holy* in the true meaning of the word. The holiest part of me. The part that belongs to my real self. I myself have no way of knowing how great it is. I suppose that many people think about this in a similar way: it is the spiritual aspect of our being that we want to protect most of all.

But writing about it has also resulted in clarity. Clarity about biographical connections, about the principles that initiated my own development and which are reliable tools for me nowadays as a therapist. And also clarity about the way I have grown and what I have learned about growth. Since the work I do nowadays is a result of these inner processes, I have decided to begin with a few biographical details.

Early Memories

My first memories go back to when I was two or three years old. I'm going for a walk with my grandma. I'm wearing a thin white dress. (I still have this dress, so that is why I know I was about three years old.)

I turn around and keep looking at my hand. Later I found out that this is a gesture in Sufi dances. I'm completely happy and feel at one with myself. As a child, I often turned around and experienced that same happiness again.

A second memory: I'm about six years old. Behind our house there is a big slope full of flowers. I'm sitting beside a blue iris, looking at it. I not only look at it, I love it and become part of it. At that time, I would never have described my experience in such a way. Only now, when I can classify emotions rationally, am I able to describe this emotion as "love."

I preserve these pictures inside me as if they belong to a dream world. And yet they are more realistic than many other "realities" in my life. They can be characterized as being coherent – they belong to this feeling of being home.

Many people have had similar experiences. Having increasingly grasped this led to my statement at the beginning of this article: we deeply know when we are home because this memory is an intimate part of us.

People who have such memories feel a continuous yearning for a spiritual dimension in their lives. In my case, I believe these memories were the driving force that enabled me to go in search of my spiritual self at an early age.

In connection with this, one aspect seems to be important to me: intuitively I "knew" that I should not talk to my parents about such experiences.

My parental home: Fortunately, I grew up in an atheist home. Especially my father, whom I loved and admired very much, made fun of religion. He did not believe in God and certainly not in any religion. The advantage for me was that I grew up without any form of religious indoctrination.

On the other hand, I would describe both my father and mother as being very idealistic. The ideals of brotherly love had a strong, formative influence on me.

Having had traumatic experiences during the war, my parents were not able to express emotions very well. One result of this was that emotional security did not exist in our family. I always felt as if I was a stranger in our house, but above all I felt that I was unloved. At an early age, I learned not to tell anyone about things that were really important for me, in order to protect those things.

For many years I imagined that other people felt at home in their parent's houses, that my experiences were unique. Mainly I thought that there was something wrong with me, that I was not really lovable. During my work as a therapist, however, I realized that this is more or less a basic requirement when you search for your own spirituality, the feeling that you are not really at home in your original family.

The Deep, Dark Valley

In my opinion, the second period of time that was important in my search for the Divine was from the age of 13 to 23. This was a very dark period for me.

When I was 14, my father died after a long, painful illness. My mother looked after him devotedly and made it possible for him to die at home. Afterwards she fell into a deep depression, from which she never recovered. As I have already said, there was no emotional communication in our family. The death of my father, my mother's depression and our inability to digest the problems that resulted from all of this caused our family to fall apart. From one day to the next, I felt as though I had become an orphan. I had hardly any relationship with my siblings at that time. I lived in another town. I also became gradually depressive, without realizing it because I was unaware of such terminology at the time. At the age of 17, I was deeply depressive and had an eating disorder. To earn my living while studying, I worked on night duty in a hospital. It was easy for me to acquire Valium there and I consumed great quantities of it. At that time, I was socially unbalanced and it seems e a miracle that I managed to recover from it all. A miracle? We tend to describe experiences we cannot understand as miracles. Nowadays I think it was the "Divine Field" that led me through that dark valley with the sureness of a sleepwalker.

In my mind, this experience is exceptionally significant for my spiritual search. Nowadays I regard that period of my life as the initial capital for my work as a therapist. With the support of the divine field, I met wonderful teachers, whom I recognized as such and in whom I confided.

The most important thing I learned at this time was that there is always a way, and it is important to set off for the road as soon as it appears. This sentence sounds quite banal but I really think there are many people who decide against moving at the very moment they should be on their way. The contents of this article will deal with this subject.

At the age of 23, my years as an apprentice began with Gerda Boyesen, a marvelous, intuitive body psychotherapist. Gradually the light at the end of the tunnel became visible for me. My awareness of life changed, my contacts became deeper and my confidence in life grew continuously. I dared to try something new and allowed new experiences to influence me.

The Long Road to Arriving at One's Goal and Becoming Healthy

The third phase, in which I find myself now, is the phase of arrival. It seems to me that there is a point in one's spiritual development when one's trust in a relationship with the Divine takes up more than half of one's awareness. From this point on, it will become easier to feel confident about life, and that's why one's real life will then often become more constructive.

At the age of about 27, I had an experience that left its mark on me. At the time I was working with my first spiritual teacher, Dina Rees. We often worked with the mantra: "God is love." That is how spirituality became closely connected with the concept of love in my life. This corresponded with my own deep desire, which has been the central theme of my life. In the beginning, I only desired to be loved. Later, it was more the desire to love that moved to the center of my attention. Dina Rees invited us to a Communion. There must have been about 300 people taking part in it. I admired and loved Dina Rees. For me she personified the sort of love I had always longed for. I was also absolutely sure of the existence of such love. Obviously, I saw her in the role of the good mother I had ached for throughout my whole life. At that time, I could already express in words what I had come to understand as my great aim in life: I want to love. At the same time, doubts tormented me. My self-esteem had improved over the last years but when my actual worthiness was in question, I still felt fragile.

So, there I was, standing in a long queue of people who moved slowly towards Dina Rees, and was at odds with myself because I felt I could not love enough. Wearing a white dress, Dina Rees was standing in the middle of the room with her eyes closed. (Maybe the parallel experience in my youth is of importance here.) When she handed out bread and wine to the person standing in front of her, she said each time: “Wine of love, bread of love.” She was perceptibly in a sort of trance, which influenced the people in the room. As I slowly moved nearer to her, I heard the words like a mantra, “Wine of love – bread of love.” As I have already said, in my thoughts I was busy with my wish to be able to love and the doubts I had concerning this. And then I was standing in front of her. But instead of saying the words “wine of love – bread of love,” she opened her eyes, looked at me intensively and said, “You already love quite well – wine of love – bread of love.” The expression in her eyes, her words and the intensity of the moment hit me like a hammer. I believe we sometimes need such moments to knock us out of the rut we have been in with our well-worn convictions. Afterwards, I felt a strong throbbing and warmth in the core of my heart. It was quite apparent that I was on a new plane of consciousness. The feeling lasted for hours. I assumed that this was the result of Dina’s words and the high regard for me, which she had expressed through her words. From today's view, I think that Dina’s words, or rather the vibration they set in motion, catapulted me for a short time into a condition in which I could understand my real self.

The heightening of one’s awareness is difficult to express in words. The person who is experiencing it has an awareness of great coherence. It was of the same intensity, the same feeling that I had already experienced as a child, but this time I was not in a dream world. At any rate, my experience was explicit. After this incident, I have never again forgotten what I am searching for, and this search has determined my life up to now.

I believe that what most effectively helped me on my way was the trust that the right way would always reveal itself. Still today, different kinds of positive experiences help me not to fight against taking the necessary steps in life.

There is always a way and it is important to go this way as soon as it appears.

The dynamics of growth are basically characterized by two fundamental principles:

- Firstly, every living thing is in constant motion. This involves an inevitable process of change or growth.
- Secondly, any motion involves a phase of instability.

The basic existence of the cosmos is guaranteed by the dynamics of motion, of process. Everything is changing all the time: Every cell contracts only to expand again. Our consciousness is also unceasingly changing, as anyone who ever tried to focus it on something can confirm.

When things change, you often experience an unstable moment. You can observe this very well from a physical point of view – for example, when you walk consciously and as slowly as possible.

To me, the phase of instability is of great interest. Unfortunately, it is seldom sufficiently taken into account, especially when it comes to emotional growth.

When we walk, we rarely become aware of this moment of instability. For one thing, we assess the safety of the path with our eyes. Furthermore, thanks to innumerable constructive walking experiences, we trust that the phase of instability is not dangerous and only temporary. This knowledge is so deeply ingrained that it has become second nature to us.

It would be a very different matter, though, if we were on our very first alpine trekking tour. Looking down to the one side, we see we are in danger of falling into a precipice. The track might be extremely narrow, stony, and damp due to the weather. Here, our confidence in safe walking would presumably vanish and we would feel insecure. Maybe we would feel it as fear, as trembling knees, as a queasiness in the pit of the stomach. Maybe our fear would be so strong that any further step causes us inner agony. Maybe we would not be able to put one foot in front of the other anymore. If somebody then covered our eyes and took our sight away, any kind of instability would cause panic or even feel life-threatening.

So, what takes the fright out of the instability when you are walking is, for one thing, the skill to create a sense of security through your eyes, and for another, all the constructive past experiences that have become your second nature and thus embodied experience. And what's more, the idea of staying in one place so as not to have to face instability would be deadly boring!

When we go through the instability phase in an emotional growth process, it feels as if we have climbed an extremely dangerous, narrow, stony, rain-dampened mountain track. We are neither aware of our inner guidance, which would show us the way, nor can we fall back upon sufficiently good past experiences, both of which would help boost our confidence to say: "I can do this!"

And even if something like a certain confidence is there, it is usually not deeply rooted. It is often just a matter of cognitive knowledge or knowledge that one has heard or read about. So, we feel for the way without being sure that we are doing the right thing. The crisis develops into a dark path; it seems as if the light is missing.

Nowadays, I think it is very easy. It is just a matter of orientation. When I am in contact with my spiritual self, it is easy to be in contact with the right orientation. But during the period after my thirteenth birthday, when I had no idea there was something like spiritual guidance – if it existed and how to contact it – life was just exhausting, difficult and, above all, lonely.

In our cultural environment, having an emotional or spiritual crisis can be particularly problematic. If you happen to be with a therapist for whom the words "spiritual crisis" is the epitome of an esoteric scene and who negates his or her own spiritual dimension, you might get very detrimental advice.

In my opinion, many patients in our psychiatric institutions are there because of a spiritual crisis. All they really need is somebody or something to show them the way because their own inner voice is leading them astray or they are incapable of interpreting it reliably.

On a physical level, we have our sense of sight and we can clearly see the path ahead. Thus, we trust in our ability to move on. On an emotional or even spiritual level, however, we rarely seem to possess a sense like that. It is definitely not a material one. And as it is not part of our "material survival kit," it takes a certain training to make good use of it.

If we are cut off from this inner sense, or are not aware of it at all, we start fighting against movement/motion and change. The phase of instability causes so much fear that we want to avoid it. We try to achieve this by either keeping up the status quo for too long or by rushing forward with too much activity, thus attempting to skip the phase of instability. In the end, neither effort succeeds.

We either turn around and around within the existing order for too long or we try to enforce an unrealistic change. In both cases, we are not in touch with our resources and spiritual powers and fall back on old, conditioned solutions. These are often found in the life-preserving survival kit of our psyche: the fight/flight/freeze responses. The whole procedure deepens, of course, the lack of confidence in our emotional and spiritual powers.

Or take a look at couples in a crisis, people who have lost their job or are going through other types of emotional catastrophe. Rather than accepting things are the way they are, we blame ourselves in these situations in a self-tormenting way: If I were a different kind of person, this situation would not have come into my life. Or we use our energy to blame others: If he/she were a different kind of person, this situation would not have come into our lives. Or we try not to see that things are the way they are by using innumerable other means of inner resistance, like suppression, denial, idealization, etc.

It all serves one purpose only: We do not want to acknowledge the change that is already visible in our life; we do not want to get involved. We try to act as if today's state is the same as yesterday's. It is this attitude that leads to an insidious process of stagnation and lifelessness and eventually to suffering.

And what we do not consider: if we cut ourselves off from our liveliness, we will lose contact with our divine self and the power we derive from it.

This behavior creates the very opposite of what we hope. It is the existing feeling of being alive that we want to keep and enjoy but instead we create stagnation, non-aliveness, and, on top of it all, painful experiences. Nature always provides an excellent balance between adequate change and adequate stability.

What do growth and change mean to people? For a tree, the matter is very straightforward – it simply grows towards its perfection. Determined by the information in the seed, there is only one way it can grow. It can become the perfect birch tree, for instance, if the genetics of the seed implies this option. Just imagine a birch tree desperately trying to become an apple tree. It might grow to be a birch in the tundra, weather- and frost-proof; or a birch in a more pleasant climate, tall and magnificent; perhaps a birch in the high mountains at the timberline, laboriously fighting its way upward: the tree's nature, however, is determined, and the tree will not rebel against it. Within its capability, it will become the best birch it can be. It will not fight its true nature.

This is what essentially distinguishes trees from humans. We possess free will. We can decide in favor of growing voluntarily, but we might just as well resist growth and the change it involves; we might even fight it. We can either make the most of the resources given to us or be in constant rebellion against the next steps to be taken. We can either grow in the situation we are in or we can hope that a different culture, religion, city, partner or job might take the growth lesson off our shoulders. We can either accept our female or male body, our age and our talents or we can project hatred and negative self-judgments on these qualities. The decision we take will essentially determine the direction and the result of our growth.

Growth and change always take place within the bounds of my true nature. I cannot change my true nature. But within my nature, I can grow tremendously, with the help of self-acceptance and spiritual alignment. This raises two basic questions: Which parts of me belong to my true nature? And in what ways do I fight it?

I am going to illustrate this with an example. Imagine a person who is very sensitive. Being sensitive often involves a fragile, delicate nervous system, which, in turn, enables the person to have deep inner experiences and a rich emotional life. These kinds of persons perceive their inner impulses very quickly. At the same time, there is a great need for space and tranquility in their unconscious; it works best in periods of relaxation, daydreaming and sleep. So, if they want to profit from their sensitive nervous system, they need to provide enough room, in a quite concrete sense, in which they can allow these very states to come into being. They will need more sleep than other people, they will have to give themselves space to let their mind flow or to meditate. If they fight themselves, for example by comparing their own rhythm of life with a high-performing partner, and then demand a similar performance from themselves, they will not be able to make real use of their nature. They will, instead, develop stress symptoms sooner or later.

Whenever we fight our true nature and prevent ourselves from making it happen, we will create destruction and suffering. Change and growth should ideally turn into a process, which can lead us to increased self-realization and a better perception of our true self. This automatically strengthens the love principle in us. We then flow with the stream of life's energy.

To me, it looks as if we only have the choice of growing voluntarily or involuntarily. The one strengthens our belief in our self-efficacy, the other leads us to believe that we are a victim of life or of others, and it creates painful experiences.

And we have freedom of choice concerning the quality of movement, that is, "how" we move on: in a constructive or in a destructive way, of our own free will or under constraint.

We do not have freedom of choice, however, in terms of whether or not growth happens. The stream flows forward. We can only fight it, we cannot stop it. We don't have the possibility not to change. It is impossible to run away from change impulses, we can only delay them or carry them out in a destructive way. This holds true for big things as well as for small ones.

This whole issue change, of moving on, is ideally a matter of how voluntarily and consciously we decide for a constructive movement, how much we say yes to it and trust that something inside will lead us the right way. If we have successfully gone through this process several times, we start trusting in our own potential, in our abilities to influence life, and thus in life itself. This in turn strengthens the love principle in us.

Constructive in this context means that our decisions are based on taking good care of ourselves and not on harming others. To decide in favor of this approach, it might be a good idea to sit and reflect upon the unpleasant consequences and the suffering we had to go through when we ignored the inner impulses for change or sat them out.

In fact, there are three energy movements that determine our life and take care of motion and change: One that creates, one that preserves, and one that destroys. As elemental forces, they shape all life and thus bring about evolution. Evolution can be described on the physical level as a constantly active force, which enables us to survive in our environment and helps us adapt to conditions over which we have no influence. On an emotional and spiritual level, it is a force that eventually – to put it in a simplified way – would like to enable us to love. So, it is a purely constructive force – but constructive does not always mean pleasant.

We make use of the *creative force* when we plan and build something new – a project, a new social network after moving house, new emotional structures, etc.

The *preserving force* comes into play when we maintain an existing order, a marriage, for example, but also well-tried working structures or a building.

We recognize the *destructive force* when things or conditions do not comply with our inner desires any more – even if we might often not be aware of it. In these cases, we set off – or often break free – to leave something behind that is no longer compatible with our present way of living.

But it also turns up when we deal with some kind of self-destructive illness. There, the status quo does not work anymore. If we want to recover, we are forced to make dramatic changes and plunge into the instability that arises with them.

These three streams of energy influence us on physical, emotional, mental and spiritual levels, whether we like it or not. They are the driving forces of our life and stimulate growth. In themselves, they are harmonic and constructive forces; if we fight them, disharmony is generated and, further on, suffering.

We do not know why or when these influences get activated. Our job as humans is to recognize which movement is currently active, and then cooperate with its energy. Only rarely are we in harmony with these life-shaping forces. At times, everything is happening too slowly, and in another moment, they seem so fast that we are afraid of losing control over our life, or life seems to go into a completely wrong direction. We barge in and fight the stream of life, mostly without questioning which constructive growth opportunities the current situation could bring into our lives. There isn't any confidence in the guiding force of our divine self.

Some Examples

In my practice, I often see cancer patients on their way to the recovery process. When I ask them about their emotional processes one to two years before developing cancer, they nearly all describe an inner state of discontentment: partner conflicts they couldn't resolve, a feeling of not being able to find self-fulfillment, an inner clarity of having to change something in their lives but not doing it, and often not even knowing what it was they would change.

Another example, which should be familiar to everyone who is in a steady relationship: Every relationship periodically reaches a point where too little change is happening. The relationship threatens to peter out. Discontent grows and spreads, and mostly the partner's faults are blamed for it. Often the tension erupts into a blazing row. If the couple then does not react to the real cause, namely the stagnation in the relationship, other arguments will follow at shorter intervals. Eventually, the relationship will fall to pieces, or one of the partners will start having an affair.

Couples hardly ever split up because they do not love each other or because they are not right for each other. They split up because they do not respond to the growth impulses adequately, and hope for too long to keep what they have. The growth impulses have been noticeable to both ~~sides~~ for a long time, but they ignored them or responded to them wrongly. Ever-growing pain is the result. When they still don't respond, destruction will happen.

What is common in all examples is a diffuse knowing of upcoming changes but at the same time a hesitation to make stress-announcing decisions or steps. They call for stress because an existing order obviously does not work anymore yet any new perspective appears uncertain, unknown and unsafe. It is through developing cancer or losing the partner that the destructive force – the stagnating field – is set in motion again.

Life means – whether we like it or not – that there continuous change within the bounds of the three energy movements. Matter comes into existence and goes out of existence. At the moment of our birth, we sign the contract with death. Happiness gives way to unhappiness, success to failure. People come into our lives and people leave us. Youth yields to old age. Everything is in constant change. In between, there seem to be phases of stability.

If you analyze why people change something, you find that in most cases their movement is the result of discontent related to suffering or destruction.

Discontentment is an important and often necessary impulse in human life for moving on. Conversely, an impulse which is ignored seems to cause discontentment. Nonetheless, the necessity to change what has been evokes fear in many people. Hardly anyone manages to recognize the impulse of discontent and respond to it with an adequate movement. This is why everyone experiences suffering and perceives change – subjectively –as something being forced upon them from the outside.

The interesting question is: Why are we so afraid of change/movement? And why do we often meet emotional and spiritual growth with fear and distrust?

I think we are dealing here, on the one hand, with conditioned emotional patterns. 'I've always got by this way' would be the common excuse. Perhaps it did not lead to the desired result but at least it led to a familiar outcome and a solution. The solution might not have been pleasant either but, then again, it was a solution on the basis of capacities that were valid at the time.

If we strive now for a different, more mature solution, it will be stressful because fears and anguish linked to the old solution will be triggered. That's why our unconscious tries to protect us from the "danger" of change by resorting to known solutions. But, as I said, this will result in suffering. Still, it seems more agreeable to a part of ourselves to bear the suffering rather than the fear of instability caused by new, more mature approaches.

If we have reacted to something in the same way a thousand times (for instance, reacted to criticism with a counterattack), then this reaction appears to be the right and proven way of proceeding. Anything else, such as listening calmly to the criticism and considering its correctness, frightens us because it has not yet been tried and tested successfully. This is undeniably an aspect of the dynamics that makes us look at change with mistrust and tempts us to wish that everything would stay as it has always been.

Furthermore, I presume that the phase of instability that accompanies every change is met with fear because in these moments, we feel threatened by perhaps losing control over our lives.

Of course, we need to consider that we recognize but a fraction of the forces we are steered by. Our sight of things does not reach any further than to allow us to rudimentarily understand processes that have been empirically examined – at least in others. On an emotional level, this refers to conditioned and therefore verifiable behavioral patterns. Our own emotional level we can only grasp in fragments, our spiritual level even less so.

If we are personally concerned, we are particularly blind to our blind spots. Even knowledge that is basically available does not seem to exist anymore or does not seem applicable to our special case.

Our biased trust in the purely material aspects of life keeps us from realizing that the source of any human change lies inside. It seems to be of a spiritual nature, and only a few of us possess a conscious, clear and, above all, trusting access to this source's field of information. That's why it seems that the exigency for change is brought to us from the outside. It leaves us believing that development is being forced upon us. This automatically stirs up resistance, at least if the imposed goods are unpleasant.

Could you, please, consider why whether the desire for change comes from within or is imposed on us from the outside is important. Perhaps it makes it easier to feel the difference if, first, you imagine your partner urging you to behave differently and, then, you decide for yourself to deal with a certain aspect of your personality in a different way.

The crux of the matter is whether you make an effort because you want to or because you have to. In the first case, you mobilize your energy, in the second one usually your resistance, which then means utilizing your energy and potential for fighting back.

Let's assume that the steps of growth are not imposed from the outside but urgently felt from within. Who or what, then, is this inner agent of development? And how can we get in touch with it in order to perceive the impulses for development more distinctly?

I would like to call it something like the guidance of the soul, a force we cannot grasp rationally but only sense and feel. For me, it is the Divine Essence in humans that keeps us moving and takes us closer to the state of love. For emotional and spiritual development, it seems essential to me to regard the Divine as part of our self; a part to which we often deny ourselves access, and which then appears to be far away from us and not taking care. We have the choice to connect with or, for whatever reasons, split away from the Divine, which we recognize as something *inside*, something that belongs to us, our birthright so to speak: if we come to such an understanding, we get access to this inner force and resume sole responsibility.

Very few comprehend the Divine as a constructive field of consciousness they can lean on in a very practical way, which operates as a supportive force in their lives. Therefore, it seems likely that a leap into the unknown accompanied by a phase of instability feels alarming. This is why many people lack basic trust in situations that require inner movement; they can't say: "I move on with courage, I respond to my challenges as well as I can and I trust that something constructive will come out of it." To put it in even simpler terms: "I do what I can, as best as I can, and my Higher Self will take care of the rest."

There is a saying that expresses the work of the Divine in a poetic way: Take five steps toward God and He takes ten steps toward you – the Divine, seen as something that goes far beyond our comprehension but can still be grasped as a constructive intelligence, a force which operates regardless of our religious faith.

Naturally, we can go on accessing the Divine as a theoretical concept outside of us and which is active without us being involved. This is what, in the end, our Christian religion conveys.

Maybe it is significant in this context that in nearly all religions, it's apparently only males who can truly understand God's nature. Male consciousness being used in a one-sided way leads unfortunately to overemphasizing the rational at the expense of being.

I find such a notion of God unhelpful for an inner quest and on the way to gaining trust in the inner voice. As long as we comprehend God philosophically as something external, we inevitably fall into the trap of a dualistic perspective. Here am I and there is God. This turns God very quickly into a personal God, a kind of super-human being, who – in ways that are hardly comprehensible – reacts to us sometimes grimly, sometimes benevolently. A force whose favor I can win through good behavior but just as suddenly lose again through something men have defined as "sin." On top of everything, we are to approach this projected God in a kind of servile submission posture.

Such inner notions of God are predestined to give birth to defiance, resistance and denial. And the sad fact that almost every religion claims to have exclusive rights on the truth, pretending that God's grace can genuinely only be won if you follow their mandatory path, does not exactly inspire trust either.

It is also necessary to take into account that nearly all big religions are imperia of power and riches. Naturally, they have an interest in seeing that people can only comprehend God through the intermediation of a clergyman. It secures their position of power.

No wonder that every fairly reflective person has a critical or even disapproving attitude towards this God. No wonder that so many people do not want to confide in this God.

To me, it seems of enormous significance to examine our own idea of God, reconsider it and free it from religious or other kinds of dogmas. To be occupied with the nature of the Divine takes us closer to our very core in the end.

In order to avoid the trap of divine projections, I consider it indispensable to regard the Divine as an inner entity. I like to refer to it as the great I, or the expanded I-consciousness, as opposed to the small I that corresponds to our own notions and the ideas we have of ourselves. Of course, the Divine field of consciousness is far more extensive.

If we were in accord with this inner field and felt its essence inside of us, it would be superfluous to ask: "Who or what is the Divine?" "Is it personal or impersonal?" "Does it work inside or outside of us?"

The Divine, applied to ourselves, taken as a superior I-entity, as a kind of inner voice that acts as a compass, guiding us through the ups and downs in life … that which sets the stimulus to kick-start a process, destroys the obsolete and preserves things worth preserving … draws what is appropriate into our life. The Divine is a kind of inner motor and compass that we need to sense and listen to, a field of consciousness that is always working for our development towards more love within the bounds of the three elemental forces described above.

It is the perfect interaction of a passive and an active principle. The active principle expresses itself in the conscious decision to turn towards the Divine Field and recognize which parts of the Divine we ignore. Following the passive principle implies listening exactly and dedicatedly to the inner voice.

All the – mostly futile – prayers we address to an external deity: we could save ourselves the effort. Instead: more listening, sensing ever more clearly, allowing the Divine plan to unfold in our soul.

I once heard of a blind woman who had learned to "see" colors with her hands. This is how I understand the expanded I-consciousness. We need to develop a sense to perceive it.

Imagine the following difference:

You have been struck by a cruel blow of fate. Maybe a beloved person has passed away, or your doctor has diagnosed a serious autoimmune disease. Or you are going through an extremely difficult situation at work and you can hardly cope with it, let's say a severe case of workplace bullying.

- You ponder a great deal why this situation came into your life. You feel at a loss and have no idea who could possibly help you. Maybe you even brood about what you've done wrong, or what you are being punished for. You wonder what life will take away from you or worry about having bad genes.
- You ask yourself in which way the situation wants to enrich your life. How the Divine wants you to mature through this experience. And you do all this with an inner attitude which says: This difficult situation will turn out to be my greatest teacher; something good will come out of it, and my inner guidance will help me in any way I need.

In the first case, you are facing an enemy. It is in the nature of man to fight his enemies. Thus, you will fight this blow of fate, you will resist it. You will take a hostile attitude towards this situation, maybe even towards life as such. With a hostile attitude towards a step in your development, you are cut off from your inner resources. You will only be able to make use of solutions stored in the parts of your brain that react to danger and threat. You will have no access to your creative potential.

Your breathing, your thinking and feeling, in short, all of your biochemical processes, will stay in stress mode. How do you, thus, recognize a solution and let it happen? In such a state, you can't experience yourself as the source of the will to change. Instead, something from the outside is acting on you: God, life, fate, your genes, etc.

A small side note: In our healthcare system, illnesses are almost always being "fought." Nearly its entire language refers to fighting something in order to regain health. This by itself appears to me to be a huge contradiction.

In the second case, you are, so to speak, a body resonating to the creative sounds of your expanded I-consciousness. This blow of fate is not directed against you. It may not be pleasant. Often there is a certain check before you make a big inner step. It wants to teach you something.

And, above all, you are not alone. Your inner voice will reliably show you the way. With this inner attitude, you quit the stress mode and become open to creative thought processes. Your intuition – the quality that enables you to sense the creative field of your expanded I-consciousness –

will let you pick up and recognize your creative impulses.

Intuition and creativity – attributes of the Divine Field – are, if you want, being fed from the back room of the unconscious. They can only be perceived in a state of relaxation. It's only then that we have access to the areas of the brain where truly creative thinking takes place. Maybe the term "creative receiving" would be more appropriate here. Surely, you know the feeling: You wake up in the morning or in the middle of the night, and suddenly, the crystal-clear solution to a problem just comes to you.

At night, our brain is in a kind of reception mode for the voice of our expanded I-consciousness. It can express itself during the dream phase and also in periods of the little-explored deep-sleep phases.

In many religious orientations, God is called "the Lord." Metaphysically speaking, this term could describe the relationship between the small and the big I: The Lord, the inner Divinity, to whom you need to align yourself and whose voice you need to listen to. The Lord as the inner voice of guidance and protection, as the divine essence, the expanded I-consciousness, which we can hear during meditation and other times of deep relaxation.

Then, words as in Psalm 23 of the Holy Bible, would gain a very deep meaning: "The Lord is my shepherd; I lack nothing..." or in Psalm 121: "I lift up my eyes to the mountains - where does my help come from? My help comes from the Lord ..." They'd lose the connotation of a patriarchal God and refer to an inner occurrence instead, which would be unburdened by God projections inhibiting development.

When we build this attitude of trust, we become a constructive, interactive, acting field of consciousness. At this moment, the blow of fate serves no more purpose than enabling us to take a step of growth towards more self-fulfillment, self-care or love. Real creativity in this context always symbolizes a bigger space, a change of dimensions: the step from the three-dimensional world into a fourth dimension, the dimension of the principle of spirit, the dimension of the expanded I-consciousness, the dimension of love.

If we are at this level of being, we experience a higher thinking, different from the one we know in everyday life. If we reach this level, we experience the world in an explicitly different form than from the level of everyday consciousness. And at this level, there is already the solution, the answer to all our troubles. That's why there is no need at all to *find* it but to *open up* to it.

There is no doubt that the voice of our expanded I-consciousness is always reliable and available. However, its information is subtle and can easily remain unheard. It takes a certain training to hear it in a way you can trust it. It grants the small I free will to follow or disregard it. Inside of us, it can be felt as a certainty.

Experiences with the Divine can neither be located in the area of knowledge and logic nor in what is provable; they represent purely subjective experiences that cannot be verified by statistical means.

To me, they are like a permanent gift from our Divine side, and demand an answer, a deed and a practical consequence.

This consequence has ultimately got something to do with the term “love.” Nowadays, in my opinion, love is one of the most overused words. I have already spoken of love several times. In closing, I would like to define it, also to avoid misunderstandings.

Mostly, when we talk about love, we talk about our own neediness and the hope that somebody else might appease it. For me, love represents a state of consciousness that can be felt as self-care on the inside and altruism on the outside. Many who have experienced love will surely agree with me that it is the most beautiful and the most important facet of a human being. Most of us know a great deal about the nature of love, otherwise we would never be able to recognize when we love another person and when this love possibly ends.

For me, love is, firstly, an energetic vibrational frequency that we can gradually come closer to by living certain human virtues, virtues that harm neither myself nor others, virtues that foster a positive attitude turned dedicatedly towards life.

As I said in the beginning: love always happens in the present. Or, you could also say that people in love aren't too much interested in the past or in the future. And we all know that living in the present is the key to happiness...

Concluding Remarks

At the end of this article, I would like to write about a deep experience of God I had in 2014. I want to emphasize that I never had the feeling that I was enlightened in any way or that anything similar had happened to me. I regard this experience as another step on my way to developing trust; trust in the Divine Field and in my own ability to comprehend the Divine plan intuitively.

For a rather long time, I had not been feeling well in my body. I tend to ignore such conditions at first but then I decided to see my doctor because I sensed that there was something fundamentally wrong. My intuition told me that it was a cancerous illness. My doctor’s diagnosis confirmed my suspicion.

I felt completely peaceful, I was not afraid and I *knew* deep down inside that this process was not dangerous. I told very few about this matter in order not to be burdened with pressure from outside. In moments like this, people tend to project their own worries and fears onto the situation and therefore also onto the person affected. I wanted to avoid that.

A few nights later, I woke up early in the morning. This is unusual for me because habitually I go to bed late and sleep best and most deeply in the morning.

I heard a blackbird singing. I have a special relationship with blackbirds and I like their song. As I felt well and cheery, I lay awake with my eyes closed and listened to the bird. Suddenly the room was brightly lit, a very special light that had an emotionally beneficial quality. I "saw" it with my eyes closed. A deep feeling of happiness spread through me. This special type of light, the brightness of it, flowed through my body. I lay completely still and abandoned myself to this situation.

Interestingly enough, my thoughts were quite peaceful. I did not have the usual difficulty disciplining my thoughts, which I have when meditating. It was not a question of whether I should surrender to this situation. Everything felt as though it was right and exceptionally coherent.

First, I felt my heart chakra throbbing. It became warm, bright and large, and then this condition spread out until it concentrated on the area where my symptoms were. There again, I could feel a strong throbbing. After about half an hour, the process was over. I felt happy and thankful and I knew that I was healthy again. The "orthodox" medical examination confirmed my observation.

In the meantime, I have told some people about this experience, but underlined each time that my attempt to describe the intensity of this experience would never be adequate to what happened. Words can never describe such a state of vibrating.

The point is that I feel a deep gratitude for the phase in my life, which I call the deep, dark valley, because in the end, it led me to this way of life. And I feel gratitude for my wonderful teachers who accompanied and led me along the way. But, above all, I feel gratitude for this power I feel and know that I can rely on it one hundred percent.

CHAPTER THREE

EMBODYING THE SACRED AT THE THRESHOLD OF LIFE AND DEATH, WOUNDING AND HEALING: THE STORY OF THE THREE TSUNAMIS

A TRANSPERSONAL AUTOETHNOGRAPHICAL REFLECTION

REGINA U. HESS

Abstract: In this chapter, different narratives of overwhelming life experiences and the experience of grasping the Divine Source, the original ground, *Anima Mundi*, the soul of the world, are woven together. The story of the three tsunamis is a transpersonal autoethnographical reflection on how the Sacred can be experienced, understood and embodied at the thresholds of life and death, wounding and healing. It weaves together psychospiritual insights resulting from overwhelming experiences of survival. A near-death experience at the heart of a major natural disaster, the loss of my mother at an early age and exposure to sexual violence in my early life each in their own way served as a catalyst for my personal psychospiritual development. From this lived-through spiritual journey, there emerged a connection with the Divine Source, experienced as homecoming, and an ongoing process of discovering our original sacred nature as a form of embodied understanding.

Keywords: Anima Mundi, consciousness exploration, embodied understanding, sacred nature, overwhelming experiences.

Introduction

In this text, different narratives and reflections on themes relating to certain personal overwhelming life experiences that I call the three tsunamis and the experience of grasping the Divine Source, the original ground, *Anima Mundi*, the soul of the world, are woven together in a story. This is not simply intended as a revelation of my own life. By exposing my heart, I wish to touch yours – or rather as they say in Hindu India, may God in me be able to touch God within you. The narratives in this chapter recount my experience of three different types of overwhelming life events, the so-called three tsunamis, that each had a very different impact on my life: Surviving a major natural disaster – the full force of nature and nearing death – in the Asian tsunami; in contrast to this, exposure to man-made violence – my early life experience of sexual violence; and lastly the loss of my mother in adolescence. Each of these overwhelming experiences connect to the core theme of this chapter related to the circle of life and death, wounding and healing, in the circle of existence. Each of these tsunami's were fundamentally existential to me. Drawing on the philosophical framework of transpersonal psychology, I reflect on processes of integration and healing in the aftermath of these overwhelming experiences interwoven with metaphorical symbolic archetypal meanings, which culminated in my personal revelation of the embodiment of the Sacred: The bodily grasping of the Divine at exactly that threshold between life and death, wounding and healing.

At the Threshold of Life and Death – Encounter with the Asian Tsunami

I was on a backpacking holiday with a friend in Thailand. We were staying on the little island of *Koh Chang* on the west coast of Thailand. On the 26th of December, I got up early, at around 6 am, and realized that there was a strange atmosphere outside. There was no sunrise. Indeed, it was unusually dark. The tide had gone far out. The birds had left. It was too quiet and the air felt tense. I had a sense that an apocalypse was imminent. I asked the locals but they had no idea what was going on either. At around 8:30 am, I heard my friend, who was running towards my hut at the beach, shouting: "Run, run, Regina!" When I stepped out of the hut, all I could see was a huge black wall of water. Within moments, the monstrous wave struck and I was tumbling under water. I could not breathe. I felt shock and a sensation of tingling and burning inside. I could not make it to the surface to take in oxygen. I lost my sense of orientation and direction. Then I experienced the feeling of letting go of my life.

I entered a tunnel of piercing white light and then saw my life in review, like in a video. After a feeling of sadness that I had to go now, I accepted my imminent death. Then I was catapulted into another dimension of consciousness. It felt as if I was entering stillness, as if the world was standing still, like a gap, a pause. In the brief moment of this deep stillness, I dove into a vastness, a caring dark warmth that bathed me. This warm darkness was like a mysterious fertile place where life is conceived; it was as if I had hit a pristine ground of love and creation. Entering this warm dark stillness, I thought that I was connecting with the nature of the tsunami's wave, as if I was synchronizing with the tidal wave. I could feel its wrathful fiery rhythm and oscillated with it. It was then that I heard a voice, as if of the tsunami, thundering at me: "I am not against you, I am with you."

The next moment I was aware of I was rising to the surface of the ocean. I could breathe again. The tsunami spat me out towards the land. I made it to the beach, and then ran deep into the interior of the island's forest. A few minutes later, I found my friend alive as well. Both poles of the experience, the near death and the sacredness of being reborn into life, were so vast that sometimes they feel as though they could blast me away.

A few days later, when I traveled from the island back to Bangkok, on my way home to Germany, I walked past miles of photographs of the people who were still missing and their significant others and friends who were searching for them. I slowly became aware of the extent of the destruction and the desperation of the masses of people in this area.

Back home, I attended psychotherapeutic sessions as a preventive intervention in order to work through these experiences and enhance my healing and understanding. They included working on feelings of guilt for having survived this major natural disaster when so many people had died, and so many families had suffered the loss of a loved one. After the tsunami survival, I realized that this encounter was way beyond the literal experience, that there was meaning in the fact of my survival and that I had a responsibility to give something to the world. I experienced a deep sense of homecoming after my rebirth out of the tsunami's womb. The tsunami encounter was a calling. I had received a calling from the Anima Mundi to dedicate my life to work around the embodiment of death and life, and the healing of overwhelming experiences, and to further support our reconnecting with the World Soul, as a homecoming to God/the cosmos/the Sacred.

Embodied Understanding and Embodied Spirituality

My understanding of the healing and transformation of overwhelming, challenging and traumatic experiences, with the aim of promoting the integration of the experience, is based on an inclusive holistic approach to health and healing rooted in the field of transpersonal psychology and psychotherapy. The core concept I draw on is the interconnectedness that assumes the dimensions of body, mind, spirit, community, culture and nature as interrelated. This concept includes the assumption that when one part of the whole suffers, all parts suffer and, similarly, when one part enhances healing and well-being, all parts can benefit from it, as described in the African concept of *Ubuntu.*

Furthermore, I place an explicit focus on the body. Our body is the carrier of our experiences. Through our body we connect with our experiences and with the outside world (Todres, 2007). Within our body, being (ontology) and knowing (epistemology) are intertwined. Language and non-linear expression such as music, poetry and art are tools that help us express our lived-through experiences, stored in our bodies. The interconnectedness of being and knowing, and the expression of experiences collected in our bodies, is what I call embodied understanding (Hess, 2012a; Anderson, 2016). Embodied understanding is non-linear – like listening to music – where the experience is much more than the individual notes.

When we are connected with the bodily sensations and bodily knowing within us, creativity, a sense of purpose and the transformation of negative thinking can be amplified. Human experiences are incarnated in the body and sculpture our bodies. Our thoughts are paired with sensations and emotions. This informs our actions in the here and now. Through the resonances of our bodily sensations, we perceive ourselves and our lifeworld. Our physical and emotional perception of ourselves and the lifeworld are based on embodiment. Cave paintings and archeological studies show the evolution of embodied human consciousness, including self-knowledge, symbolism and, later, written language.

More Than Language Can Express

Finding the ability to give expression (Hess, 2012b) to some layers of the implicit, the more-than-words-can-say, appears to me to be one important element in integrating into the Self overwhelming experiences, including those of psychospiritual crises and psychological trauma, and enhancing embodied understanding, integration and healing (Hess, 2012b).

Creative methods resonate with our aesthetic sensibilities and as non-linear expressions enable us to access what we cannot utter, the more-than-words-can-say – the implicit, which nonetheless looks for words to be expressed. The aim of using non-linear aesthetic expressions (Hess, 2012c) such as poetry, art, metaphors and archetypes is to move understanding forwards by transcending the limits of language and finding expressions that touch us and elicit the implicit meanings, rather than with the linear expression of the rational mind alone.

After the tsunami encounter, I felt suffering and pain because of my inability to express the dimension, complexity and profound elements of this overwhelming experience. Stretched between the two poles of a continuum with the near-death experience at one end and the experience of tapping into a sacred space under water and being reborn out of it at the other. Years later, some of the multiple layers hidden in the experience of my tsunami survival began calling for excavation, whereas others remained invisible and deep in the world of the inexpressible. The ongoing process of experimenting with different forms of aesthetic and non-linear metaphorical expressions for certain aspects of the phenomenon has enabled me to communicate some layers of the experience, and this has brought me relief. At the same time, there is a feeling of vulnerability in relation to the depth and sacredness of the experience, as well as of personal disclosure. It is the listening to the layers of the experience that needs careful and loving midwifery whilst allowing space for the silence of the unspeakable.

A few years after my survival, the muse of poetry visited me and *transmitted* a poem to my consciousness:

in the tsunami's womb—embodying a universal rhythm
…demons and angels submerged with me in the tsunami's womb...
    captured by the wave
    fearing death
    seeing my life's story passing
    negotiating: *it is too early to go*
i am not against you—thundered the voice of the great mother—*i am with you*
    tumbling *into a tunnel of light*
    saying good-bye, the pain of letting go
    sadness and grace streaming through my body
we are your guardians—whispered a choir of angels in my ears
hearing a sound of pure love
    embodying the rhythm of death and life
    the universal rhythm of all that was and ever will be
    embodying my destiny
    born into a new life out of the tsunami's womb… (Hess, 2007)

Some time after the poem emerged, two metaphors relating to my tsunami experience occurred to me. Suddenly, I understood the tsunami as a trickster – the *trickster archetype*, who often appears in myths as a radical transformer – mirroring the radicalism that I encountered. The trickster keeps us from being too sure that we are in control: He is seen as a deconstructor as well as a creator of worlds; he dissolves all boundaries and embodies both polarities, and he crosses the line, breaks the rules and undermines duality. The trickster appeared to me as inhabiting the natural power of the tsunami, not only with its destructive but also its transformative energies of creation. To me, the 2004 Asian tsunami was just such a (r)evolution: the world upside down, beliefs shaken up and new roads of understanding of life and death opened. It addressed our mortality within the cycle of life and death.

The second major metaphor that eventually emerged was that of birth. Returning from the threshold of death was like being reborn out of the tsunami's womb, with the archetypal image of birth and of the tsunami as Mother Earth or the Great Mother birthing me. The ocean was like the amniotic fluid in the womb of a pregnant woman. Being reborn out of the water of the tsunami can be seen as a spiritual dimension of birth at a universal level, in the sense of *being born out of the cosmic womb's sacred waters of the Great Mother*.

In the process of understanding and integrating the layers of my experience, a third core metaphorical image appeared: *the sound of the silence of the more-than-words-can-say*. What remains as an infinite feeling when I contemplate my tsunami survival is the acknowledgment of a realm of the silence of the unspeakable and inexpressible. The unspeakable realm of my tsunami experience calls for *a space of silence, a space of just being, a space of stillness and peace*. I experienced a profound shift in awareness when reflecting on the deep silence of the tsunami. It felt like a timeless place, a space of sacred stillness, like being at peace or being peace itself through connecting with an essence that felt like love. When I gave more space to the silence, rivers of tears flowed. A desire emerged to honor the dead, including those who had died in the tsunami and its aftermath, and our ancestors: "Walking, I am listening to a deeper way. Suddenly all my ancestors are behind me. Be still, they say. Watch and listen. You are the result of the love of thousands" (Hogan, 2012). I felt as if I was hearing a voice calling me to build a memorial or a temple dedicated to the *sacred silence of the inexpressible*.

The power of this sacred silence brought forth another important metaphorical image, that of darkness seen as an expression of the eternal pristine ground of life. After the tunnel of white light when nearing death,

I feel as if I had dived into a warm fertile space of darkness, a primordial ground of creation where life is conceived, or symbolically incarnated in the grounds of the cosmic uterus. Darkness can be seen as the depth of the earth, the cosmic womb of the Great Mother, as a receptive and nourishing energy that can deliver life. Darkness has a silence and depth, a stillness and peace. It can lead us into the mysteries of creation and existence when we enter the unknown and not-knowing. I experienced a deep sense of homecoming, a coming home to the source of all creation after my rebirth out of the tsunami's womb, and a reconnection with the Divine Source that I call the *Anima Mundi,* the World Soul.

At the Threshold of Wounding and Healing

During this book's gestation, the authors went together on a group book retreat. Our goal was to dive together deep into a space of connecting us with our spiritual nature and our writings, and indeed a feeling of coming closer to God emerged in all of us. I felt that our connectedness was enhanced by the spirituality of the place we spent these days: Mariastein Abbey, a Benedictine monastery on a mountain in Switzerland. Deep under the monastery church, in the stones of the mountain beneath the earth, is a natural cave shaped like a sacred womb. It is a sacred place, worshiped as a manifestation of Mary, the Mother of God. The sacred site has been a place of Marian pilgrimage for several hundreds of years and is invested with a strong Divine Feminine energy that we all felt and connected with. We spent time in meditation in this sacred space and experienced precious revelations and transformations of our book chapters during our time there. An atmosphere of love, warmth and divinity filled the space within and around us.

While we were reflecting on and discussing my chapter, my co-authors were struck by a certain phenomenon: They had a sense, a feeling, a question about what other overwhelming experiences, literally asking (and thus inspiring the title of this book chapter) what other tsunamis might have happened in my life before the survival of the Asian tsunami. I was dumbfounded. Although I had never spoken about this with them before, it was true. I did not want to reveal those experiences and tried to hide the stories about the other tsunamis. The confrontation was very challenging and at first, I felt that I could not speak about what it was. I was standing on the threshold of giving voice to the secret of my other wounds, the earlier tsunamis in my life. It was so difficult that I almost despaired, but at the same time an inner feeling told me that it was time to cross this threshold. It was a deep desperate struggle, a back-and-forth movement of being unable to speak and yet wanting to express what had emerged in the deeply shared sense-field of our group. I decided to take this step forward and cross the threshold of the silence. It felt like a bungee jump. First, I spoke about an earlier tsunami in my life, which was easier to talk about, the experience of losing my mother when I was 14. Then came the most difficult, the fact that even earlier in my childhood, I had experienced sexual betrayal. For many years, I had worked on it and integrated these experiences. Other than my therapists, only a handful of close friends knew about it. But in recent years, something had changed within me and I felt it was important to end my silence. Even today I feel shy, ashamed, and do not want to be identified as a victim of sexual violence. Speaking about this with my colleagues was now another level of opening up. It initiated a process of transformation that led to my decision to express these experiences of tsunamis here too, embedded in the deep journey of writing about my experience of coming home to God or coming closer to the Divine (Feminine) Source.

In the tsunami encounter in Thailand, I experienced the threshold between life and death, accompanied by an overwhelming sense of oneness with everything. It is easier for me to talk about the experience of near-death experience than about the sexual violence. The experience of sexual betrayal was a man-made trauma, which made it very different, as has been the process of healing. Having shattered my trust, it is closer to me. The wounding is more invasive on other levels of experience, such as my bodily integrity as a human and as a female child, and later as a woman. Its impact, such as feelings of being intimately harmed, disrespected, uncared for, unloved, was potentiated by the early death of my mother.

My mother died while I was still an adolescent, and I became suicidal. I felt overwhelmed, desperate, and was at a loss to know how to move on in life and how to manage my life. But there was always a sense that I was surrounded by something, some kind of energy or spirit that wanted my well-being, that wanted me to live my life in happiness and contentment and fulfill my destiny. It often felt as if I was hearing a song of God, with a choir of angelic voices singing lullabies to me, as though they were nursing me and soothing my wounds. This kept me alive, enabling me to step back from suicidal thoughts. Something in me was sure that suicide was not to be my path and step by step, I regained the ground under my feet.

I often compare the experience of wounding to the pearl that evolves out of the wound of the shell. It takes a long time for the pearl to fully emerge. That is how the long healing process and integration of the sexual wounding into my Self feels to me. Through the process of therapy and healing, and deep support of close friends, the wound became one of my strengths, the strength to be vulnerable, touchable, sensitive, with a wealth of empathy and compassion for the wounds and suffering of others. This in turn led to my work as a psychologist and transpersonal psychotherapist. Helping wounds to heal, particularly those related to the intimate feminine, plays an important role in my life and in my work with female clients. It is also a way of honoring the Sacred Feminine and working on the healing, integration and balancing of the Divine Masculine and Divine Feminine principles within us and our world.

I feel that Nature has given me a strong healthy body with which to hold and transform all these experiences, along with a large portion of resilience and a strong indestructible link to the Divine Source that has enabled me to immerse myself in a continuous healing process, out of which pearls have grown. I feel very grateful for this process. And I feel that whatever happens in my life, I will get back on my feet and move on and develop further. It seems it is one part of my calling in life to have the capacity to feel and hold suffering, not only for me but also for others and for our world, and to enhance healing and resilience through empathy, love and compassion, in order to transform it into embodied understanding and further awakening of consciousness, to be concerned with the preservation of life, of all life, Mother Earth and beyond.

Other Altered States of Consciousness and Transformative Experience

Not long after our author's retreat, I went abroad with a guided group and participated for the first time in a shamanic sacred ceremony using the psychotropic substance psilocybin. During the guided ceremony, I had an experience that somehow brought together, in a very condensed form, all the pieces of my life that I am writing about here in this book. In an expanded state of altered consciousness during the shamanic ritual, I felt that a voice was speaking to me: "You are now entering the process of dying. Be aware of every second of this dying process so that you can let go of everything." I traveled through different scenes of tremendous human suffering, such as war, executions by the Inquisition, mass rape and murder. These were collective pictures of death, wounding and human suffering. At one point, I seemed to zoom in on a picture and saw myself forced to lie on a table, bound by my legs and arms. The atmosphere in the scene was like that in pictures of torture. I saw myself and many other women being raped and tortured to death. Yet, during this same shamanic journey, I realized: This is the past, I am alive in the present and have no bonds. I am healthy. I am free. Once again it was as if a voice spoke to me: "Yes, you are free. Get up, move on, and do what you want and need to do in your life right now. You can develop your full power and full potential now. You are ready for it. Do not hide anymore. This is over. A new chapter is beginning. You are the power of the earth and you are the stars of heaven. You are connected with the center, the Divine Source." After embracing this message, still in the expanded state of this shamanic journey, I got up. Standing on my feet, filled with joy, bliss, love and eros, my arms, legs and hair in the air, I danced wildly, fiery, passionately.

Embodied Understanding and the Principle of Energy Flow

Neurobiology and neurophysiology have shown how traumatic memories are stored in the body and thus confirm the importance of including the body in the transformation of trauma. The focus must be on the connection with the body and on gaining understanding of emotions, thoughts and spiritual experiences through this bodily connection. Working with the body through body-mind-spirit practices can have a ripple effect on well-being because it affects all dimensions of how we experience ourselves and the other in the world. Using our body's innate wisdom and capacity to heal can be a valuable tool in the process of healing and transforming challenging experiences. The body is the vessel that holds our experiences, and through our body we can directly access our experiences as embodiment and embodied understanding, including the implicit and unknown, by tapping into the borderlands of consciousness. The healing process involves the disintegration and reintegration of experiences to incorporate each new insight into change and transformation. I perceive energy within and around us and in the cosmos as the underlying and unifying principle based on interconnectedness in the process of healing and transformation, as well as of the expansion of consciousness (Hess 2012a).

Energy can be seen as the life force called *chi*, *ki*, or *prana*, depending on the cultural background. In the context of holistic health and healing, energy is assumed as flowing when the person experiences a sense of wholeness while, when the energy flow is obstructed, physical, emotional and mental imbalance results. The principle of energy flow can be found in traditional healing systems in diverse cultures – such as traditional Chinese medicine, acupuncture, Ayurvedic medicine, meditation, Yoga and the martial arts. Energy is understood as a specific force in nature and in the human body where a balance needs to be maintained, for example, through certain practices for the body, mind, spirit and nature. *Body-mind-*

spirit practices – such as Tai chi, acupressure and meditation – are seen as energy-based exercises that promote harmony and wholeness in the body, mind and spirit. In my doctoral dissertation (Hess, 2012a), I investigated the impact of the so-called *Capacitar Training* for the transformation of trauma with body-mind-spirit practices. Its aim is to assist the release of traumatic stress and increase the energy flow in body, mind and spirit. Subsequently, the same principle should be applied to the individual's role in the broader aspect of community and environment as formulated in Capacitar International's (U.S.) motto: Heal yourself and then support the healing of others and our planet.

Bodily and spiritual experiences are intertwined with each part (e.g., each person), being fundamentally a part of the whole (cosmos), as described in the following:

> The call of embodied spirituality is to learn to access the truth of our own dignity, and to infuse all aspects of reality with this awakened attention – beginning with our own bodies, and extending into the greater bodies of family, community, culture, country, humanity, the earth, and the cosmos itself. Our embodiment begins with ourselves and gradually extends outward to heal the world. (Caplan, 2007)

Indigenous peoples in the Americas explain trauma as "fright paralysis" and as "soul loss" that needs to be healed through shamanic rituals (Levine, 2010). The healer and the person seeking help join to re-experience, for example, the traumatic event, while calling on cosmic forces to release the energies of demons that might have entered the soul during the trauma event and calling back the lost parts of the soul. This is another approach to healing and transformation. It relates as well to the community aspect and the importance of nature in the realm of healing, as emphasized by the Capacitar approach. The shaman's knowledge is used for the welfare of the community and harmony of the cosmos. It is humanity's oldest spiritual tradition and can be described as a science based on experience.

Conclusion

The threshold of life and death, wounding and healing, has been an important recurring theme in my life and feels like a catalyst for the development of my psychospiritual awareness, including altered states of consciousness. With every encounter, I understand the phenomenon in a deeper and more complex way.

My encounter with the 2004 Asian tsunami in Thailand, the experience of being exposed to mass destruction and the trauma of the people there, and my own development through this nondual experience, was a major turning point in my personal and professional life (Hess, 2017). Through the tsunami experience, everything was shaken within and around me. It was a shock, but at the same time the experience of the world turning upside down had an ongoing transformational impact in the sense of movement and growth. Over time, I encountered changes to, and insights into, a spectrum of nondual consciousness and its border zones. I experienced a non-physical space, filled with light when nearing death, and a fertile pristine ground of warm darkness when returning to life. Even now, years later, I can bodily connect for tiny moments to the experience of these realms at a level of what I refer to as *borderlands states of consciousness* (Hess, 2012d). It is an experience of oneness, as a state of non-duality, as if everything is an interconnected whole. These memories are stored in my body, and through my body I can connect with these experiences. The experience of nondual borderland consciousness is an embodied understanding of the interconnectedness of ego, Self, others and nature within the border zone between consciousness and unconsciousness. The idea of nondual embodied understanding as a borderland state of consciousness allows us to place trauma, including transgenerational trauma, not at the individual level only but rather within a perspective of interconnectedness that includes culture, the collective and nature/cosmos, and as such embodies the connection with the Divine.

Along the way, I have experienced overwhelmingly challenging stumbling blocks as well as most wonderfully blissful enhancing experiences that have enabled me to thrive. According to C.G. Jung, only after our mid-life transition, based on self-work, self-transformation and self-realization, does our real self, the true authentic Self emerge. "Life really does begin at forty. Up until then, you are just doing research" (Jung, 1961). Somehow this is how it feels to me. For several years now, my conception of my experiences has been different. I feel like I have become a witness of the story of my past life instead of being an actor in it. I less strongly identify with past experiences and feel that I am in a process of becoming freer and that my true Self is unfolding. I feel great respect and gratitude for the impact that time has. As simple as the saying "time heals all wounds" sounds, I still feel it is profound. The healing of emotional wounds takes time. The healing process has its own time and its own rhythm. It takes time for the fruit of healing, or the pearl of the wound, to be ready for harvesting. Only then can the wound leave the past behind and enter a new cycle of life. Only then can a Gestalt find closure and a new Gestalt begin. For some years I have sensed that I have entered a new cycle of life, living much more detached from my past, and thus bearing with me all the rings of the tree of life that I have and that I am.

In my own process of healing, understanding and integrating overwhelming experiences, I have found spiritual practices such as meditation and prayer, and body-mind-spirit practices that enhance the energy flow to be beneficial. They can heighten the feeling of interconnectedness and evoke a sense of coming home to the source of all life. Finding a voice and non-linear aesthetic expression for layers of these experiences seems to me an invaluable gift.

During my nearly 20 years of therapeutic work with a vast number of clients with different overwhelming or traumatic experiences, I have found that embodied spiritual approaches to healing can have a positive impact that can bring us closer to the threshold where we can connect with the Divine Source. I feel thankful for my soul's path to and across the thresholds that can enable transformation and healing. I am grateful for the chance to accompany my clients on their soul's path and their journey of reconnecting with the Divine Source. Being the guide in this process feels like a homecoming, too.

The impact of major disasters such as the September 11 terrorist attacks (2001), the Asian tsunami (2004) and the Natural and Nuclear Disaster in Japan (2011) and so forth can shatter the lives and beliefs of the world's communities. In the aftermath of disasters, there endures prolonged distress not only in the individual but also in the social and communal context. Vulnerabilities and risk factors are part of the human potential, as are protective factors such as resilience. Transcendent beliefs may provide meaning and purpose. Traumatic events and experiences can profoundly affect the body-mind-spirit integrity of the individual within the social and communal context and may predispose one to either greater resilience or greater vulnerability to the interpersonal, social, political and environmental stressors in our lives (Hess, 2017).

Individuals and societies cannot just "bounce back" to a "pre-disaster state of being" (Walsh, 2003). Perhaps a more apt metaphor for facing unanticipated future challenges is to anticipate the healing process as a spiral movement. An overwhelming experience can be a wake-up call, an epiphany to reorient priorities in life and gain compassion for one's own sufferings and struggles, as well as those of others. Such a turning upside down of the world moves us beyond the realms of the literal and the logical towards the borderlands of our consciousness and our lifeworld. Such a turning upside down of our lifeworld may initiate a moment when the veil of creation lifts to reveal the Divine Source and the sacredness of our being.

From a holistic integrative perspective rooted in the field of transpersonal psychology, the human experience of death, life, wounding and healing impacts the holistic dimensions of body, mind, spirit, culture, community and nature. Individual well-being is assumed as intertwined with community, ecological and collective well-being. Healing practices for the individual and community rituals may enhance the connection with and expansion of embodied understanding. This in turn can further the healing of overwhelming experiences including individual wounds and community and transgenerational trauma, and contribute to the well-being of the greater whole. It is important to evoke and support the natural and creative process of healing that can be assumed as innate in all human beings (Levine, 1997).

The life force – *élan vital* – can be imagined as a web of life in which all entities of the cosmos are interconnected. It is innate in our body, mind and spirit, and so intimately connected to our well-being that the world cannot be perceived as a battlefield or a trap, but rather as a larger Self or the *world as a lover* (Macy, 2007). We are like a living part of a living whole, or a cell of the Earth and beyond.

By embodying the cycles of death, life, wounding and healing and their thresholds, and connecting with the universe, we can grasp the Divine Source. Coming closer to God, or coming home to God, in that sense, is the embodiment of the connection with the Divine Source or the cosmic soul, the ensouled world that Hillman termed the *Anima Mundi* – the Soul of the World, what Heidegger named *der Ur-Grund – the primal ground,* and what Meister Eckhart meant when he wrote: *the soul is not in the body, the body is in the soul:*

embodying the sacred
heartbeat of the universe
returning to the center

at the threshold
eros of love
splendor.

(Hess, 2014)

References

Anderson, A. (2016). The transpersonal research colloquium 2015: Reflections on hermeneutical, embodied, and arts-based approaches to research. *Journal of Transpersonal Psychology*, *8*(2), 140-149.

Caplan, M. (20007). Walking the talk: The principles and practices of embodied spirituality, in J. J. Prendergast & G. K. Bradford (Eds.), *Listening from the heart of silence.* St. Paul, MN: Paragon House, p 181-186.

Hess, R. U. (2007). Unpublished poem. Santa Cruz, CA, USA.

Heß, R. U. (2012a). Women's lives in the U.S.-Mexico borderlands and their experiences with the 'Capacitar Practices' for transforming trauma: An Embodied inquiry. Retrieved October 9, 2012, from Proquest (U.S.), Dissertations & Theses / Open Access: Full Text. (Publication No. AAT 3529762).

—. (2012b). Beyond the Abyss: Re-born out of primal waters:' An autobiographical embodied understanding of the phenomenon 'surviving the 2004 Asian tsunami'. *Journal of Archetypal Studies, Vol. 2,* (U.S.), 121-135.

—. (2012c). Poetic embodied interpretation of re-search findings: an evocative approach to social sciences methods. *Creative Approaches to Research, Vol. 5*(2), (Australia), 20-33.

—. (2012d). Nondual embodied understanding as 'borderland state of consciousness': Relevance for theory, practice and research in transpersonal psychology," *Integral Transpersonal Journal, 2*(2), 80-96.

—. (2014). Unpublished poem. Cologne, Germany.

—. (2017, forthcoming). Disaster mental health. Intertwining a transcultural transpersonal psychology perspective. *International Journal of Transpersonal Studies.*

Hogan, L. (2012). *The secrets of joy: A treasury of wisdom*. Philadelphia: Running Press (1995). Retrieved on July 27, 2012 from http://www.lovehealth.org/books/joy

Jung, C. G. (1961). *Memories, dreams, reflections*. NYC, NY: Vintage Publishers.

Levine, P. (1997). *Walking the tiger: Healing trauma*. Berkeley, CA: North Atlantic Books.

—. (2010). *In an unspoken voice: How the body releases trauma and restores goodness*. Berkeley, CA: North Atlantic Books.

Macy, J. (2007). *World as a lover, world as self: Courage for global justice and ecological renewal.* Berkeley, CA: Parallax Press, p. 30

Todres, L. (2007). (Ed.). *Embodied enquiry. Phenomenological touchstones for research, psychotherapy and spirituality.* New York, NY: Palgrave Macmillan.

Walsh, F. (2003). Crisis, trauma, and challenge: A relational resilience approach for healing, transformation, and growth. *Smith College Studies in Social Work 74*(1), p. 57.

CHAPTER FOUR

COMING HOME – OR THE PATH OF FAILURE

STEFAN DRESSLER

Abstract: Although we are always eager to be successful, we keep experiencing moments and times of failure in our lives. We like to hide these moments of personal failure from ourselves and others. But when we dare to encounter ourselves in them, the space inside of us and around us can open in a way that can change our lives. It is in this way that eventually we can encounter the Divine.

Keywords: change of life, coming home, encounter the Divine, path of failure

What is the Divine? Coming Home or the Path of Failure?

In our culture, God is scarcely present in our everyday lives, and even then only secretly. It is not easy for me to write about the Divine. What or who is God? What is the Divine in me, what is it in the world I live in? And what does it concretely mean to me in my most daily life? I do not really know who God or the Divine is. To write about this feels presumptuous. It is extremely difficult and, at the same time, one of the most important questions in my life. God is incomprehensible. So far away from myself.

I recently had a mystical experience. It was a masculine experience, of being an erotic man, fully enjoying my male body. With an open heart, feeling immeasurable love, singing and dancing, embracing myself and the world. I saw a huge golden cathedral, the golden Jerusalem on a hill, radiating in beauty up into the eternity of heaven. There was immense beauty and love in this light and in this inner image, within me, in all human beings, and in the world around me – a beauty that was seen, heard and felt. I was feeling rich and fulfilled, with solid masculine roots, my heart open, connected – much more than connected – striving and yearning towards the golden Jerusalem, to the Divine.

I felt as if I had a taste of what it means to encounter the Divine in me and all around me. I felt very comfortable within myself and with the world around me. I felt warmth, trust and peace. And I was completely free of fear.

Coming Home

But such meaningful moments do not last. They will fade away again. We do not come home just once, like in the experience I just described, and that's the end of it.

In this state of being, inwardly coming home, I sensed what it meant to touch the Divine. Even though I thought I sensed it essentially, my mind does not completely know what the Divine is. God does not have a name. In the Tao Te Ching by Lao Tzu (1989), it says: "A being that can be comprehended is not the being of the incomprehensible."

As a human being I can have experiences through my senses with the outer world around me and with my inner consciousness. I will be able to send experiences that approach a deeper truth, the place where something feels, appears, sounds and tastes "divine." What is necessary in order to get there?

First of all, I must be *me.* The more specific I am, the better. This does not refer to what I am thinking at this moment but rather to who I am in my body, my sensations and my feelings. Without the body, without this starting point, I cannot perceive what is in me and around me. I can easily get lost in my mind's projections and concepts. Noticing my feelings inside me helps me to discern my perceptions (i.e. distaste or agreement).

Being in the present moment... In contrast to the part of our mind that likes to worry about the future or get hung up on the past, conscious perception and inner agreement can only occur in the present moment.

A kind of inner authority is required, which consciously decides to be aware and perceive and can then focus inwardly on a certain object. Through this inner authority, I open myself to the present moment.

To me, it seems important that after a certain period of suffering, one that is felt *physically and mentally,* the perception, the feeling of inner agreement and openness to the present moment deepens. The perceptional filters (the inner resistance) decrease. How tremendous is the view from the mountain *after* the long climb. How wonderful does a simple glass of cool water taste *after* feeling thirsty on a hot summer day. But only if I do not simply guzzle it down. Pausing and being consciously slow is also helpful.

You can try this yourself. Take all these points into account and focus on an (ideally interesting) object. Ignore your mind's complaints and then, after a while, if you maintain a level of inner awareness, you will sense an inner balance. Your perceptions come closer to the Divine when they are in balance and reach an air of completeness (not of perfection) – regardless of whether the object is a symphony, a single note, a cathedral, a Madonna, a painting, nature or a wonderful time with friends. This only works when you *feel* connected. The inner complaint stops and within yourself there is only a "yes" without a "but." You stop wanting to go somewhere, to have, or not have, something.

I do not *know* if what I touch here is *really* the Divine but at the very least, when these elements come together, it *feels* good, deep within myself, either for short or for long periods of time. Good in the sense that everything I need in life is present. I become still, content, happy within me and I feel at home with myself. I believe that I feel at home with myself thanks to this conscious perception, thanks to a certain effort (being aware and personally motivated) and after having created a personal connection to a perceived object. This can be a subtle sensation or an overwhelming experience.

Unfortunately (or luckily), we keep losing this sensation of agreement and closeness to the Divine – the experience of feeling at home with ourselves. As if in a current, we drift away from the present moment, from our present physical sensations, from the sense of connectedness to something in us or around us. Even though we do not want to go away (once we have been there), a kind of inner distance or alienation can quickly develop, a separation of two parts within us. One state of consciousness drifts further and further away but, nevertheless, does not cease to attract us. It will soon unfold its own drama. In the other state, we might still remember feeling at home.

The distant state (as a part of our self) becomes practically invisible, incomprehensible, as if in a fog. We cannot take an inner objective distance to this part because we *are* this distant part. I am convinced that the part of us that is further away is yearning to reach the other part, to come home and be happy. Yet we identify primarily with the distant part. Very few people are aware of this. It means we are unhappy deep inside, unhappy with ourselves and with the world, separate from ourselves and others, and we feel stressed or pressured. A lot of people in our culture feel this way.

In many spiritual traditions in which inner experiences play a central role, such as Christian contemplation, Yoga, Zen or other Buddhist paths of meditation, it is vital to become stronger than this current trying to pull us away from our center. This must happen through conscious action.

You can fight this current with discipline (which is certainly important when one follows a spiritual path) or/and you can ask where the current is pulling you. I think this is an interesting question. The current is pulling you away from home, from your center, and leads you constantly to failure in spite of your goal of being happy. It pulls you into a daily *drama.* Into a daily *inner* drama that could be hard for you to leave, and might remain unconscious if you are relatively successful in life. The drama seems normal, it is just the way you are. Everyone constructs his own personal drama by giving himself, and others, similar roles. This drama becomes more visible within moments of failure during inner and outer (life) crises, strokes of fate or illness. *Without us noticing this – since we tend to make outside circumstances responsible for our failure –we find it difficult to recognize our own responsibility.* Along our inner path to the Divine, failure is the rule rather than the exception. Failure appears to be an essential life experience.

Where is the current pulling us and what does it have to do with failure? Let's assume that the inner current is pulling us into a kind of everyday drama that becomes very intense in moments of failure.

Failure, the shadow of success, is dealt with in contradictory ways in our success-oriented culture. When it affects others, we find it fascinating. Tabloids thrive on stories of failure. Once it affects us personally, we find it difficult. Our personal failure is taboo. No one likes to talk about it even though everybody knows it and fears it. On the surface, it appears as if we all aim for success but if we review the statistics, it becomes clear that we actually create a secret culture of failure: 90% of all German citizens wish to die in their home but about 85% of them die in hospitals or special-care homes; 85% of all adults wish for a satisfying and fulfilling partnership but only 20% say they have one. If we look at the business world or sports, all that counts is to be number one or to be the most successful, but if the competitors were honest, they would have to admit that only a very few of them reach this objective.

When it comes to failure, it is also important to look at the perspective we take when we feel in a state of failure. If wealth and money are the most important assessment categories, then they create very different measures of failure in life than if the main goal is to be content (and money is only marginally of interest). Inner perspectives and assessment categories change throughout one's life. Things you thought made you successful when you were young will possibly be valued quite differently later in life.

What Exactly Does Failure Mean?

In an ideal world without failure, you would have a need, a wish, a plan, a life script. Whatever else this might be, it is definitely an impulse you present to the world you currently live in. You become aware of this impulse, express it, put it into action and thereby fulfill your wish (need, plan, etc.). The result is an inner relaxation and contentment. Then the next impulse appears. And so on, as long as we live.

Every impulse that you bring into the world has a goal. Unfortunately (or thank God), the world is full of obstacles, obstacles in the outside world and in the inner world: Some needs and impulses (i.e. the need for a partner, relaxation, a new job) have been repressed either briefly or for years or dare not be voiced at all. Or we voice them and encounter a "no" or difficult circumstances (e.g. the ice-cream parlor is closed). If there is no outer obstacle, we might not dare put our wish into action because we fear the consequences (a conflict, an embarrassment or a long-cultivated illusion might die). Our fear is there simply because we are (or always have been) too "convenient."

If an obstacle comes up, we try to push it away or get around it. If we do not manage to do this, we fail to reach our goal. We can apply this to our whole life … whether it is the wish for raspberry ice cream, a partner, less fighting, a better job, sex, needing to pee, sleep, a whole life script or anything else.

Obstacles come from outside or from within us. You might mainly look at the inner obstacles because you think you can influence them. And they often have an impact on outer obstacles. But no matter what kind of obstacle appears, the lack of fulfillment and the inability to realize important impulses, needs or plans will always lead to inner tension and discontent in the long or the short-term. *Always.*

This happen, whether you are aware of it or whether it remains unconscious. When it comes to physical needs like needing to pee or feeling thirsty, this is easy to understand. If we do not fulfill these needs, this will lead to increasing tension until we become aware of the tension and take action. If we wait too long, the situation can get out of control.

When it comes to the need for closeness or sexuality, it is already more difficult for some people to become aware of the tension and discontent that builds up when they cannot fulfill these needs. For couples, this often leads to the dynamics of constant subtle criticism between the partners in everyday situations. If you are in touch with yourself, you might be able to see this tension in direct connection with the unfulfilled (important) need. Otherwise, perhaps you only feel an unclear physical tension that you cannot relate to the unfulfilled need or plan. And sometimes there is no awareness whatsoever of the tension until a strong persistent physical tension or pain is felt.

This tension is at first felt on an energetic, emotional level (e.g. in the form of discontentment). After a while, it is also felt on a physical level (e.g. neck or stomach pains in the case of suppressed anger). In the course of their lives, every person builds up tension in various places of their body and soul, from small to large tinderboxes, ready to ignite when the occasion comes.

We yearn for a release of all this tension that has built up in us. In reality, we yearn for openness and change in order to grow inwardly. *Theoretically.*

If it were not for the donkey. The donkey is a part of this drama into which we are constantly being pulled. The donkey has four legs, which give it stability. The donkey is smart and stubborn. The donkey refuses to accept change. And when it does, then it only permits small, manageable portions of change in life. The drama usually unfolds when we are touched in a critical place where we have gathered a lot of tension. This feels like a sore spot, a wound that has been hit. Then things become serious. Maybe not for others but certainly for us. Feelings of guilt and shame become predominant on the inner stage, often in combination with failure, weakness, anger, pain/mourning, or fear and even panic. At this point, our self-confidence becomes unsteady. Sticking to our metaphor: the donkey stumbles. Stumbling is usually not too bad but we hate to fall. Thus the donkey immediately tries to get back up on his four legs. As fast as possible. We do not want to pause and become aware of what is happening within us. Think about it. Remember a situation in your life when you felt hurt, when you were ashamed or when you failed, and how quickly you wanted to get out of there.

There are two preferred strategies for inner stability. The first possibility is to withdraw or hide (get out of the difficult situation). This can happen inwardly by becoming stiff or silent, trying to look normal, explaining yourself somehow, smiling stiffly, resigning, sinking into shame or self-blame, etc., or outwardly by running away. Personal expression and assertion yield to adaptation or are completely abandoned. One feels like a victim. The inner question that revolves in one's mind is: "Why do I always fail?" Frequent withdrawal from everyday life and conflicts often end in burnout, depression or at the very least in a kind of resignation and discontentment. I call this kind of self-confidence stabilizer "permanent failure."

The second possibility is to begin to fight with the world and with what or whoever hurt you; you become angry. Personal expression and assertion become over-emphasized with the ambition to control the world or your counterpart, to dominate to the extreme of wanting to destroy. I call this type the "never-fail." The inner question here is: "So there! Why should I be the one to fail?" It is not really a question but an inner attitude based on arrogance. Psychologically speaking, this is often a form of narcissism. Never-fails come to psychotherapy very late or not at all, and if or when they do, the situation is already very serious.

Despite their differences, both types maintain three strategies:

1. "I am the victim"
2. "I am right", and
3. "Whose fault is it??? Definitely not mine!"

These three strategies are often present in everyday life for many people in our culture, even without moments of failure, but then they are usually quite obvious. Many politicians, most of whom are "never-fails," are true masters of these three strategies. These strategies protect us, especially by conquering shame and guilt. And, most importantly, we do not have to change ourselves at all. Those are the advantages. The disadvantages are that others do not like to listen to us when we are caught up in this attitude. We also make ourselves invulnerable, untouchable in relationships with others. This annoys others even to the point of infuriating them, depending on how long we last. But the most essential disadvantage is that we give others all the responsibility and thus continue to replay the same inner (and outer) drama. One could say that type 1, the permanent failure, allows – without being aware of this – too much of himself to fail (and in doing so does not allow the part to fail that really wants to do so. I will come back to this later on). The never-fail tries to prevent himself from failing at all.

What is crucial is that both types want to change the world and not themselves. The permanent failure does this secretly and usually manipulatively; the never-fail is more or less overt. But the rest of the world does not permit this, or at least not all the time, not even when someone has a lot of money and can create an environment that almost makes it appear as if he were successful in it.

Both types secretly want to remain victims, which is why I call both positions "failing as a victim." We like to take both positions, sometimes we take on one in our jobs and the other in our private lives; sometimes one of these inner perspectives is dominant in all walks of life. But when things get difficult, almost all of us generally choose one or the other. If we maintain this attitude for too long, at work or in private, then at some point we will collapse: "major failure." Most people sense it coming long before it happens; we sometimes just wait for it to happen. This has a lot to do with our donkey that has such a hard time with change, especially when it is connected with uncomfortable feelings and consequences. We would much rather stay within our comfort-zone and blame others for our failure.

Both paths lead ***away*** *from the feeling of being at home with one self.* Both paths lead to a kind of defiant undercurrent of accusation of the environment, partners and God. Both paths are chosen in order to avoid feeling the emotions of failure because we are afraid to lose our inner stability, control and orientation. There are numerous inner strategies and distractions to get away from the point of failure. We use almost anything – TV, music, sex, meditation and so on. In the long run, both paths are doomed to failure. In both cases, we are fighting the wrong battle.

Paradoxically, the fastest way out is straight through the fear, into the difficult emotions. The donkey immediately becomes stubborn when he hears that.

The first step is to not routinely and quickly as usual get through that first moment of failure, but to pause. Pausing and recognizing is a **priceless** inner moment with painful and shameful feelings that permit a deep inner truth to shine through. Change the perspective from an outer to an inner one, away from "who is to blame," "I am the victim," "I am right" to doing nothing at all, pause and wait, and be with yourself. Be with your insecurity, confusion, fear, shame, guilt, etc.

A change of inner perspective is unavoidable. Without a new look at the situation, you cannot see the way out. Instead of asking questions as a victim, we need inner questions that help us take on **responsibility.**

1. "What part of me wants to be *seen*?"
2. "Where am I *blocking* myself?"

and, most importantly,

3. "What part of me *really wants* to fail?"

Furthermore, the way out demands a decision; the decision to see one's self, to want to meet one's self in the moment of failure. It sounds harmless but there is a lot involved. We squirm and trick. The decision has consequences for us. And the path that will unfold requires courage. The greater the feeling of failure, the more courage is required and the more consequences ensue. But the moment of failure is also the moment the inner figure of the hero appears. The inner hero's power is always a little bit stronger than the fear we feel.

When we decide, we face the fear of meeting ourselves in the moment of failure. Then and only then, the hero in us appears.

The three questions mentioned above refer to three inner figures: figures according to Gestalt therapy (Naranjo, 1993; Rebillot & Kay, 1993/1997) or the inner stage (Reddemann, 2001), which I would like to describe further and which are helpful for the inner work in moments of failure. Inner figures are, as I understand and work with them, inner parts with their own voices, feelings, sentences and gestures. They are constantly being recreated and changing but they also have something that withstands time within us, like the figure of the inner child, the inner critic, the warrior, etc.

The Sore Spot in Failure

Let us first take a close look at the moment the sore spot is hit. Like I said, first, there is the figure of the donkey, a part of us that does not want to change anything. The donkey always wants to present a specific version of us to the rest of the world. The donkey represents how we think we ought to be. We have worked hard our whole lives on our donkey-self. It originally developed as a creative and intuitive reaction to certain environmental conditions and relationship experiences that hurt our basic needs. Attitudes like "I must be strong and manage alone" are a reaction to an environment that, early on, deemed feelings such as sadness or pain as weaknesses. Sayings like "boys don't cry!" or "be a good boy!" are a reaction to an environment that often blames and criticizes. The donkey-self has survived many upheavals and has been tested countless times in close relationships. And most importantly, the donkey-self gives us orientation: "This is the way I am and this is who I am not. I am right. And what do you know anyway!" That's not something we are willing to give up. The donkey is faithful, he is always there for us and he always strives for a maximum of inward or outward recognition.

In the moment of failure, when our sore spot has been hit, when things become serious, the donkey runs away (we lose our familiar stance) but immediately tries to return and pull through with the usual habits and routines. This might not work because the inner tension is too strong. The pressure that has built up (often over years) and now wants to be let out is too much. In this case, a new figure shows up on stage. It is at first hidden and does not show itself in full form. The cocoon that covers it is made of fear, guilt or shame, or most often all three. It is the *hidden figure. We do not want* to reveal it, neither to ourselves nor to others. Thus – along with this figure – another one appears. I call this third figure the demon, in accordance with Rebillot and Kay (1993). The demon wants to stop or hold back the part of us that wants to reveal itself. The demon is the inner figure, the inner power that wants to prevent us from being our full selves. This blocking inner force is an essential part of our self as a whole and is a constant, generally invisible companion in our everyday lives. The demon wants to be in control. The demon always seems to be superior when he reveals himself, especially in moments of failure. We are afraid of him, to the point of panic and agony, in contrast to the donkey, who also loves to be in control. The demon has some similarities with the donkey but they are magnified, in their purest form. The demon keeps the part of us that wants to reveal itself in the shadows. It is a force that is at odds with our vivacity and our deeply glowing truth at this stage of life. Usually, the "doomed battle" I mentioned before begins at this point. It is doomed because this fight normally leads to everything remaining as it has been. Except for a great deal of gloomy excitement (uncomfortable shameful and guilty feelings, the feeling of failure, etc.), nothing happens. The demon has reached his goal, and the hidden treasures that appeared for a short time – in larger crises for days or weeks – disappear back into the depths of our soul. This is the usual course of events.

If we pause and ask ourselves the three questions mentioned before, interesting things happen. At first, it can be frustrating for many people because "there is nothing there" except unpleasant emotions and physical reactions. But they are the important thing here, as well as the *hidden inner figure* and the *demon.*

In order not to become too theoretical, I would like to explain this with an example. Years ago, a man came to me for therapy. He was about 60 years old at the time. He felt like a failure, a loser, and he no longer wanted to live. After false accusations from his boss, he had broken down in fits of tears. Since then, he had felt incapable, was agitated, lacked concentration. He kept making mistakes and had a hard time getting up in the morning. He had never had problems like these before. *Major failure.* He told me that he had been trying in vain for many months to tackle his work. He had an executive position in a large business. The actual situation had been preceded *by frequent minor failures:* it turned out that in the last year, he had worked late hours at the office, beginning early in the morning, 12 to16 hours a day, on weekends as well. Without any time off for a year. He blamed his wife (felt misunderstood and pressured by her demand for a holiday, etc.) and himself, especially his body that would no longer function properly and gave him headaches, sleeping problems and stomach aches. He was strained without noticing it and felt helpless.

He was also completely exhausted, which he could (and would) barely register. He felt like a victim. His work (which he really liked), the business, his bosses, his wife were all to blame. *Failure as a victim.* His donkey-self was principally occupied with mental concepts such as "first work, then play," a strong sense of responsibility towards the business: "I must... but I can't... ." When his boss severely criticized him, all the pent-up tension, which arose out of his unfulfilled needs for physical equilibrium, closeness and security, was released. The donkey's habitual routine (pulling himself together, holding out) stopped functioning.

The hidden figure that emerged was one of a small boy searching for love and recognition, who just wanted to be held. This figure particularly identified itself with his body and was visible to others, but not to him at first. He simply did not want to have this figure and the associated emotions (shame, guilt, failure and weakness); he rejected them completely. The role of rejecting was taken by the *demon.* It gradually became evident that the demon who rejected the needy part in him and pushed for achievement was especially connected with his father and an internalized paternal voice. The false, futile battle was to continue the denial (represented by the father) of the inner hidden figure (the needy little boy) and to work hard at being a good boy. This good little boy was secretly afraid of the father in the past and his authoritative bosses in the present – instead of getting into the necessary conflict and saying "Stop, I won't do that, I am angry," etc. A change in inner perspective was essential so that he could step out of the drama. He needed to take the side of the hidden figure, the little boy with all his repressed feelings (anger and pain) and go into the inner conflict with the (long-dead) father, who, at first, he believed to be invincible. From the perspective of the little boy, this is a perfectly normal view. It demanded courage to rearrange his life goals, which had been working hard without recognizing his own boundaries and the physical need for relaxation in order to fulfill the subconscious yearning for his father's appreciation. The change went into creating more sympathy for himself, especially for his weaknesses, establishing clearer boundaries and recognizing his need for close relationships.

A part of his donkey thus changed and made room for something new. The adopted ideals, which had in truth been his father's, needed to fail and die. So did the fear of the invincible father of his childhood, who, one could say, had driven him into this crisis – or at least into the most important aspects of it. This painful realization was the sacrifice he had to make. If I look at the whole process, I'd say that after his failure, going through his whole inner conflict and, finally, mustering the courage he needed in order to take up the battle of his inner figures, he had come home to himself.

It demands a lot of courage to face the inner fear. In his case, it was the fear of failure, to do something wrong and then be punished by a withdrawal of love and by the father's contempt. His fear of failure changed into love and more sympathy for that part of him, which had been rejected the whole of his life.

Courage is the most important of all the values on the spiritual path.
(Mahatma Gandhi)

This transformation, you see, does not occur without sacrifice. It always requires an inner hero. Without him, it cannot take place. Why?

In order to face the fear and become able to tackle the conflict with the demon, a breaking of taboos is necessary. The hidden figure that we reject is at first vague, unclear and foggy, something we want to hide from ourselves and the rest of the world. It needs to be illuminated and examined. We need to discover what or who it is and learn to accept it. In our example, it is the little boy and the adult man of today who can recognize and respect more and more of his needs. He must see the demon with whom he had subconsciously identified and learn to embrace the donkey that had put all his energy into suppressing, hiding or even abolishing the vulnerable man who, in truth, wanted to show himself when he failed.

Failure is useful for getting connected with and confronting a part of ourselves that has been separated, in order to reintegrate it. The part of us that we reject in the moment of feeling a failure is the very part that we need to integrate and accept. The part of us that does the rejecting (among other things) is the one we identify with, and this part wants to die. This is the exact opposite of how the donkey thinks and how he wants things to be. Failure also connects us with our own personal wound, the one we normally try to ignore.

The taboo in our example was, on the one hand, "I am not allowed to be angry or to see my father as a difficult person. I might lose his love and his acceptance because he'd feel hurt and withdraw and thus punish me." On the other hand, the taboo says: "I am not allowed to feel and recognize what happened to me (in my childhood)." Because of these taboos, my client was not able to be aware of his needs and the boundaries in his daily life, and he was not able to fight for them either. *Since he does not feel "at home" in himself, he was not connected with himself.*

In such a therapeutic process, there are usually several taboos (crying, expressing anger, accepting help, etc.) to be overcome. In retrospect, they are all usually connected with one another. A taboo always contains a very personal, intimate aspect. Something that is a taboo for one person might seem trivial and easy to do for someone else. A taboo is always caught between two extremes. On the one hand, in order to protect social interactions, it must never be broken. Otherwise, there could be severe punishment, mostly love deprivation, loss of membership in a group (i.e. family) or even death. On the other hand, breaking a taboo has an almost magical appeal for us.

Countless fairy tales deal with this aspect. Take Bluebeard, for example: Shortly after marrying Bluebeard, who is the rich but somewhat sinister lord of a castle (and has a blue beard), his new wife, the heroine of the fairy tale, is given the keys to all the doors of the castle. She is permitted to enter all rooms except one, which has a very small key. She must not open this door under any circumstances otherwise something horrible will happen. As soon as the lord has gone – she cannot wait for him to leave – she opens the forbidden door and the story takes its course. We always expect the taboo to be broken when we read these stories. Always. We would be very antsy if the story ended without finding out what was in that room.

Breaking a taboo feels like treachery to the person doing it and to the family or group that wants to maintain it. In one's experience, a taboo is generally covert, which means that one is not aware that it needs to be broken; the thought is quite foreign. When a taboo is broken, it sets a great deal of energy free. – energy such as vitality, creativity and joy.

The guardians of the taboo are mortal fear and the fear of going insane.

People who are almost ready to take this step and then take it tell of feeling they would die or go insane if they continued. They must get past these two guardians. They do not know what will happen afterwards. It is not up to them, though the donkey wants to know the answers to these questions in order to maintain control. What happens afterwards is never under our control. Otherwise it would be cheating and we would be pretending. Life changes after breaking a taboo. In some extreme case, events may unfold that we cannot control and that change our life completely.

In the fairy tale, the heroine finds women's corpses in the room, Bluebeard's former wives, who had been killed. When Bluebeard returns, he immediately asks for the little key, which is covered in blood because she was so startled and dropped it in the room. He wants to kill the heroine for breaking the taboo. Then one thing leads to another. When the heroine gives up her role as the victim, she finds a way out of an apparently unsolvable situation and dares to take on the conflict with Bluebeard, who is killed in the end. She inherits his fortune and marries a "highly respectable man" (Kast, 1998).

As long as the identification and the split are not conscious, as long as they command us inside, the same drama will continue to play itself out with every failure. It will continue until the inner balance tips and heads into major failure. In the previous example, the situation became unbearable for the man's donkey-self, the client became completely enveloped in the rejected part of himself (the inner child with his regressive needs). This is why it was so hard for him to deal with it. The inner tilting to the part that is rejected happens if we ignore certain needs or wishes for too long or adhere to unsuitable life scripts. The tension becomes unbearable and needs to be released. For the person affected, and for those around him, this is usually hard to deal with because a part of his personality that had remained hidden from others (and often himself) until then takes over. From this perspective, manic, depressive and psychotic states suddenly begin to make sense.

Generally speaking, our minds identify with the rejecting principal, the demon, and our bodies with the rejected part, the hidden figure. The body can withstand this patiently for a long time using body tension or, more specifically, body armor (Lowen, 1993). The earlier in childhood the part that "visits" us at the point of failure was separated or rejected, the harder it is, and the more time it takes, to recognize this figure in all its facets. We also need the hero in order to allow the deep pain of the inner child, the strong anger of not having been loved and having had our basic needs neglected. It is a challenge for us to permit this rejected and needy part in us to surface completely. The more we do so, the more we stop being a victim. This is an inner process that often takes years.

The demon can be symbolic for the negative parental interjects (internalized voices, parental views) but also, on the spiritual level, for negative dark beings or even evil itself. Paradoxically, it also feels like an inner release and healing when you identify with the figure of the demon, and become able to express it emotionally and physically. This can happen and is being fostered in the protected setting of holotropic breathwork, for example. It is as if this blocking principal first has to be experienced completely within you so that its power over you is lost.

Changes such as new solutions do not take place if you try to find a new way to deal with the situation but rather completely ***become*** *that which is unbearable.*

All these moments of major failure (the breaking of taboos, accepting the rejected part of me, the battle with the demon, the identification with the demonic principal) during which we need the hero are processes of death and rebirth.

In these moments of death, we show our vulnerability, take a risk and face our fear. In these moments, the donkey gives up and sacrifices control. These moments are not conscious decisions, they simply occur. They are moments of humility and dedication. The old part that was blocking us in life fails, and something new develops. What this really means only becomes clear in the period following such inner processes.

Instead of being a victim, feeling like a victim, it is important to make a sacrifice. Without a sacrifice there can be no true change in the old drama.

If we are ready in these moments of inner death – and we really can experience this as dying, e.g. during holotropic breathwork, see images of death and rebirth right up to an emotional and physical sensation of death – we can encounter the Divine. The hidden figure that emerges sometimes seems so powerful that sweeping changes in our personality structures occur that go much further than in the example I have described here. In this case, we refer to this process as the death of the ego. In such situations, a deep opening to one's self often takes place (which is felt subjectively as an opening of the heart). There might even be an entry to the spiritual dimension; you might have intense experiences of light, Kundalini-processes and many others.

In my view, it is also important that we stay in the process of minor failure for a while, regardless of whether we are in the position of victim or in a more self-responsible manner. We need time for the inner figures to be created and their meaning to become clear. We also need real psychological strain, a proper push, otherwise the donkey will never be ready to leave for another pasture. It is as if energy wants to accumulate at the place of the inner blockade in order for us to make the leap to the next level. During holotropic breathwork, it becomes evident on a physical level, often for spectators as well, that energy collects in the area of the blockage before something new is revealed. After the dense moment of inner death, the solution becomes visible.

The entire inner process unfolds in several phases during every mental crisis, every failure, and every inner and outer healing process.

1. Being/living in familiar structures.
2. Being stuck in the battle with the part that wants to be seen but which we reject: failing and feeling like a victim. The tension gradually increases.
3. Tension is released, the peak of major failure. The hidden figure and the demon come on stage. A sacrifice is needed that feels like death. The hidden figure is integrated and transformed into the

blocking principal, the demon and a part of the donkey.
4. Something new is born, and grows.

These four phases correspond to the perinatal matrices, as Stan Grof (1998) would say. They can be equated to the four phases of natural birth. In my opinion, this is an important fundamental, inner procedural dynamic that, unfortunately, has been neglected by conventional psychiatry and psychotherapy. I remind you of depression treatments primarily aimed to aid the client to function again in their familiar old structures (back to the first phase), ignoring the fact that this is an inner dynamic our soul must go through in order to reintegrate the missing part. And which especially ignores that there is something that wants to fail during depression, that wants to die. The depressed person misunderstands the level of dying. Suicidal thoughts are reduced to prevent the individual from actually committing suicide (which, of course, is very important), but the topic of death is not really integrated into the therapy. They wonder why the depression keeps reappearing and call it “recurring” depressive syndrome. During the course of our lives, we constantly encounter our underlying problems and *must* fail at them in order to reach deeper/higher levels.

Jung once accurately wrote about the shadow, the integration of the hidden figure: “The shadow is a moral problem which challenges the entire ego-personality since no one can become aware of oneself without the immense moral effort of the shadow.” And: “One does not become enlightened by imagining figures of light but rather by allowing darkness to become conscious. This latter process is unpleasant and thus not popular.”

Here I always see the Divine shining through – in me and in my work with people. These are heart-touching moments, the moments of failure in life, moments when someone pauses and reveals himself in his shame and what enwrapped it for a long time (sometimes decades), moments of breaking taboos, moments when someone dares to feel and show a deep pain or allow their strongest anger to emerge. These are moments when our shadows reveal themselves. Shadows, the unloved parts of us, of which we have many. So many that we spend the time of our lives to integrate them. As long as we reject these shadows, we must project them. Then we appear to be whole again but only through the projection of that which causes pain in us and our environment. These moments, when we go through our fear, however big or little it may be, these moments *open our hearts* for ourselves and for others. This, for me, is the sense of failure.

In every person's life, there is usually one central problem they turn around and around, fail, have breakthroughs, fail again. A problem that keeps making them despair, which wears them out, and with which their heart gradually becomes softer, more open, wider, more compassionate – to themselves, to others, to children. A problem which, if they don't give up, gradually brings them home.

The path of failure is in its crucial moments also a lonely path. As a child and well into adulthood, I stuttered; countless times I could not utter the words I wanted to say, often day after day. Through this I experienced failure in the form I now call *minor failure*. With feelings of shame, guilt, loneliness and defeat that I only felt vaguely beyond diffuse suffering. In it my inner figures appeared daily, in a fog, but whose true meaning I could not see for many years. I felt very much like a *victim*, fought for many years the doomed battle against stuttering, identified with the rejection, with the *demon*. My *donkey* developed, adapted and withdrew inwardly and externally and worked hard not to say or do anything wrong. Until, with different life circumstances, I developed enough independence and dared to take on another perspective. And felt stuck experiencing *major failure* when I realized that the life script I was living at the time was not really my own. I stopped being a victim getting ready to make sacrifices, to go through the fear. Began the good battle for my inner truth, breaking taboos inside of me and in my family, against the *demon*, who was also fed by the negative parental voices in me. Breaking taboos had far-reaching consequences in my life and my close relationships, consequences I could not foresee. One of the essential outcomes was that I felt much closer to myself, to my personal truth, to my emotions, and in my body, I felt more at peace with myself. And was then more and more able to build an appropriate and fulfilling life for myself. *I came home more and more often.* I also noticed that I was not alone with my suffering. And I slowly started to embrace the *hidden gestalt*, the rejected part, the little boy and the stuttering. Up to this day, I embrace myself when I fail and feel ashamed, and this touches my heart. When I succeed in doing this, I feel at home.

So, what is the Divine, what is God?

The path of failure shows us who we really are. In moments of failure, our heart is touched and we touch the Divine in us, whether we notice this or not. We can hurry past these moments or we can allow these priceless inner moments to come close to us. If we continue on this path and advance into ever deeper layers of our self, look at what we are hiding, what we are afraid of, what we identify with completely and then let it go until the next failure, the next inner death, then we grow inside, become wider, more compassionate. Level by level (Wilber, 2000).

The path of failure is a spiritual one. And an honest one. At some point or another, we all fail in many essential areas and topics of our lives. Failure can also serve as a corrective for our overblown ego. It teaches humility. People who tell about their biggest defeats responsibly and with dignity, not as a victim, touch our hearts. Failure in life lets us become more adult, more mature in dealing with our obstacles, with other people and with ourselves. At some moment, we must responsibly face up to what wants to show itself to us, whether we want to or not. We can postpone failure but we can never prevent it, even if our donkey is ever so clever. Without failure, we would all have delusions of grandeur. Without failure, there is no growth towards inner peace, contentment and compassion with oneself and the rest of the world. There is no coming home, no meaningful encounter with the Divine, no development of consciousness. And at the end, as I gradually begin to comprehend, there will always be love, deep compassion for ourselves and others. In retrospect, I can say that these moments of failure have been the most valuable ones in my life.

I am just wondering how it would be if all the people on this planet really faced up to their *minor failure* in daily life, and at some point to their *major failure.* The futile battles with themselves and the rest of the world would come to an end. Oh, how many hearts would open, the Divine radiating and no longer veiled by fear.

The golden Jerusalem on earth. In us.

References

Bellinger, G. (1989). *Lexikon der Mythologie* [Dictionary of mythology]. Germany: Bechtermünz Publisher.

Campbell, J. (1979). *Der Heros in tausend Gestalten* [The hero with the thousand faces]. Germany: Suhrkamp.

Caplan, M. (2002). *Auf halben Weg zum Gipfel der Erleuchtung* [Halfway up the mountain – The error of premature claims to enlightenment]. Petersberg: vianova Publisher.

Gilmore, D. (2007). *Der Clown in uns* [The clown inside ourselves]. München: Kösel Publisher.

Grof, S. (2000). *Psychology of the future. Lessons from modern consciousness research.* New York, Albany: State University of New York Press.

—. (1997) *Kosmos und Psyche* [Cosmos and psyche]. Frankfurt a. M.: Krüger publisher.

Jaffe, A. (1971) *Erinnerungen, Träume, Gedanken von C.G. Jung* [Memories, dreams, reflections of C.G. Jung]. Olten: Walter Publisher,

7. edition, p. 414.
Kast, V. (1998). *Abschied von der Opferrolle* [Farewell from the victim role]. Freiburg i.Br.: Herder.
Levine, P. (1998). *Trauma-Heilung* [Healing of trauma]. Essen: Synthesis Publisher.
Lowen, A. (1993). *Freude – Die Hingabe an den Körper und das Leben* [Joy – The dedication to body and life]. München: Kösel Publisher.
Naranjo, *C.* (1993). *Gestalt Therapy: The attitude and practice of a theoretical experientalism.* Nevada: Gateways Publishing.
Rebillot, P., and Kay, M. (1993). *Call to adventure: Following the hero's call.* San Francisco, CA: Harper.
Rebillot, P. and Kay, M. (1997). *Die Heldenreise* [The hero's journey]. München: Kösel Publisher.
Reddemann, L. (2001). Imagination als heilsame Kraft [The healing power of imagination]. Stuttgart: Pfeiffer / Klett-Cotta.
Lao Tzu (1989): Tao Te King. München, Wien: Otto Wilhelm Barth Publisher, 8th edition.
Wilber, K. (2000). Integral psychology. Consciousness, spirit, psychology, therapy. Boston, NJ: Shambhala Publications.

CHAPTER FIVE

GOD AND THE LITTLE EGO

VITOR RODRIGUES

Abstract: This text hints at personal experiences, personal changes and ensuing reflections on their context and meaning as they brought to the author's life the theme of God or a God-like power. It describes how the author was forced to deal with unexpected issues such as "psychic attacks" or the presence of the Divine in his life. Also, it brings on some non-ordinary matters such as possible traumatic effects from seemingly very positive experiences or the opposite, gains from experiences with darkness, or the apparent power of prayer.

Keywords: dark, God, light, prayer, presence

Introduction

The proposition was clear and surprising: writing about God and my relationship to Him/Her/it (as I cannot find any way to define a gender or a category to "God." Do we mean "He" or "She" or "it"? Doesn't God supposedly include everything?). I never before considered writing about such a momentous subject. Then I felt enthusiasm about this. Please note that "enthusiasm" is a word from the Greek "en" and "theos" and means being "full of God." Or Divine force. But I cannot say that I am full of Divine force as I start writing. I cannot feel it directly as such at this precise moment even if I feel "enthusiasm" and have a happy heartfelt smile as I start. Warmness, love and peace are here.

A First Experience

My first experience with something close to a feeling of the Divine happened when I was about sixteen years old. By that time, I was in love with a young girl who did not correspond. So, one night I was wide awake in my bed, thinking about how unfair this was with some sadness. And then, suddenly, the sadness became acute despair, a feeling that I could not stand, it wasn't possible to live like this. I felt enveloped in darkness and it felt like darker than the absence of light. Then I noticed that this darkness wasn't coming from within: an overwhelming dark force was dragging me into what felt like a black hole and I could not resist it. I was interested in esoteric stuff and parapsychology but all of it was outside, in the realms of intellectual speculation. I believed I was agnostic. But now, feeling how I felt, a silent cry came from within me: "God, please help me!" It took one split second: I felt a flash of intense white light over me, so large and intense it felt like the whole town had been touched by it. Immediately afterwards, my room was quiet and warm. I felt peaceful, noticing that even the normal darkness of the night seemed to have become clearer, as if a sort of diffuse light was now in the particles of the air. I knew it was over and I knew I had been protected. No fear, only a nice feeling. From that moment on, my agnosticism became knowing that both negative forces and beautifully powerful positive ones did exist.

Later, I discussed the way everything had happened and I know that moment marked me and produced some trauma but also a deep trust in Divine realms; some duality but also a deeper longing to expose myself to a higher wisdom. After this, during many years, I felt attacked at the psychic level by a lot of strange, aggressive entities. That literally obliged me to follow a severe discipline of meditation and psychic protection. I felt that I would die, become mad or learn how to protect myself and really apply it with energy and determination. I *had* to learn. During those years, I could be hit at almost any level of my personality structure. It could be my body, suddenly feeling drowsy, lacking energy, feeling strange pressures over the places of the chakras, feeling sick or about to faint and so on.

It could be my emotions, suddenly or progressively feeling angry or sad, fearful or obsessed by some repetitive thought, suggestions of images corresponding to angry ghosts, dark monsters… it could be my mental **state**, feeling confused, out of focus, slow, "closed" and so on. I was aware of what seemed to be demonic attacks, vampire attacks, and many from just "normal" ghosts. I was obliged to observe how and when they hit me and at what level. I learned that some "weakness" from any personal unfinished business would be used against me at any time. For example, jealousy could be turned into anger and even despair; fear could become acute insomnia.

But I also learned that no attack could really hit my soul. So, the quest for my soul and the Divine became also necessary because of that: at the same time, I was longing for the Divine, I knew that the higher I could raise my consciousness, the more at peace and free from fear I would get. But I had to pay close attention to and explore my personal issues as they were used against me one by one. The inner child from the past, afraid of bullies, had to be dealt with or he would just become terrorized by psychic attacks; the lonely adolescent had to learn how to resist the forces that cried: "You are alone and nobody will help you."

These experiences trained me to be helpful to many clients who had similar ailments, many times with good results. They still help me with many clients. However, things have changed a lot. I will get back to that.

A Cosmic Trip

Years after my very first experience with what seemed to have been a helping hand from God, I had one powerful, deeply meaningful experience that opened me even more to a sense of the Divine. I will describe it later. Then, throughout the years, I had many other "smaller" experiences. And always this inner knowledge that there is a presence beyond words or descriptions, beyond understanding, beyond space or time. Nothing is more intimate in me and in anything or anyone else. All my effort, all my spiritual practices since then have been an attempt to come back to God. I also came to feel and know that the little ego is but an illusion and an obstacle and that to come back home, the ego is not the real traveler. Something in me is the traveler.

My first experience had been, to some extent, with "negative" and "extremely positive" forces that felt external to me. Then, one day, some thirty years ago, I was meditating. Suddenly, an unknown feeling of "acceleration" and dizziness manifested itself and it felt like I was going through something out of the ordinary. Not knowing what it was, I resisted. Then it stopped. By that time, I had received training in the art of receiving "psychic messages" and so I received one. It said something like: "Son, like this we cannot work with you. Next time, feel it and, if you don't find anything against from your inner being, let it be. Don't resist the experience."

I felt almost ashamed and I felt that I had failed to feel more deeply. But, fortunately, the next day I had a new chance. While meditating, the same feeling came back: acceleration, dizziness, as if something, an invisible force from outside/inside, was about to overwhelm me. But I felt nothing wrong with it and I allowed it to be. I felt in total clarity that the deep sounds of my physical, emotional and mental bodies, together with my whole human personality and my soul, were together. I could feel and know each one of them although they blended in harmony. Then I did not go out of my body: something in me jumped out of Vitor Rodrigues, simultaneously out of body and mind. Vitor was no more; that illusion was no more important than a grain of sand on a giant beach.

But something was present. In a way, I felt the answer to the old question about life after death as "There is no death. I have always been and I will always be." My mind felt distant and, in a way, paralyzed. Something infinitely different was now here. Now reality had been reversed and my usual concerns were but a faraway illusion. I had been sleeping and my normal, everyday consciousness was unconsciousness. Now reality was here. I had crossed the threshold into something absolutely beyond doubt. The whole space-time was something I could move into or get out from. I had a distant perception of my many previous lives as a human, but they seemed to be all simultaneously present, as if in a necklace. I had the perception of the center of the planet and the beings of light in it, among them the "Youth of Eternal Summers" and the Masters of Wisdom who seemed to be abysses of pure light beyond their human appearance. The feeling was indescribable. And then, later, I came back without knowing why or what for. During this state of consciousness, there was no need, no point in coming back. Nothing was necessary, everything was complete. And at the same time there was this feeling of Presence. No sense in saying that it was in me or out of me. It was Presence. Then, suddenly, I felt a snap at the base of my spine, something went up, and an incredible rush of light and power appeared in my brain. It was like a stadium light had been lighted inside my head. It felt just too much, I could not endure it. I was afraid it would destroy my brain and I did my best to stop it, feeling that someone was helping me from the outside. After some moments, it stopped. If felt as if it went back down to the base of my spine. I relaxed, started moving… then a sudden, similar burst of energy came again. This time I could still stop it and then, for a time interval I cannot detail, I did not dare move even an eyelid. After this, very, very slowly, I moved. Nothing happened. Another movement, very slow. Nothing again. I returned to my normal, mundane life. I had come back to my brain and body without wanting to, and it also had felt like my brain could not process the experience, a vastness like the whole internet for someone only possessing an old mechanic typewriter to write it all.

Later and in the years to follow, I could recall some other aspects, as if they were still slowly filtering to normal consciousness. I know I was fully aware of the way animal consciousness was still a big part of my usual functioning, and the fact that in my heart, a mystic cross of very high energies and lower horizontal ones was happening.

"Divine Trauma"?

When I came back to being Vitor Rodrigues, I was sort of surprised, because when Vitor was no longer there, there was no point in becoming him again. There was no point even in becoming part of space and time. For years, I did not dare mention this experience that felt so sacred even to my closest friends and spiritual practitioners. But much later, I noticed a sort of residual trauma and its effects: it was as if my brain cells and my body, not to mention me as a human being, had become just too afraid of "extreme light." So, many times, in meditation, I would feel something important like a light rising, a flow of energy, a new perception or intuition, even states of relative bliss… and I would just come back from meditation minutes later and start reasoning about them or taking some notes. This was okay, but part of it was the product of the fear of "too much light."

Now I know we must "stay there" and allow the experiences of light to unfold and transform us at the most intimate level of our body and soul. This takes some daring and, of course, trust in God above us, above our understanding and both our desires and fears – and with some discrimination to be able to do this only towards the "real" Divine. So, I am teaching even my body and brain cells to accept the light.

At the same time, I became aware of the way our animal nature may act sometimes. I have observed monkeys who have before them a whole table full of all sorts of food but then they run to it, grab a bit and escape hastily to their corner to eat it, even turning their backs to other monkeys as if afraid that someone could steal their meal. Indeed, in meditation, I did many times what now seems to me quite similar: I touched on the light and, instead of staying at the table and benefiting from the whole banquet, I escaped with a tiny candle to my corner to "process the experience." Why? Fear of too much light. One only learns slowly and carefully how to dive and accept diving into more than this. Perhaps even to jump into the Divine fire Rumi (2003)[i] told us about…

Of course, I often wonder intellectually about God. Do we know it exists? Can we even try to understand it? I would answer yes and no. Let us see what can happen when our mind tries to grasp God. We guess it must encompass the whole universe, don't we? OK. So, if God

---

[i] Translations and commentary by Coleman Barks.

encompasses the whole universe and is in charge of it, one must conclude that in a way this amazing vastness of galaxies is his body. But then, if we take the analogy further and if we believe *speed* to be a limitation in the universe, we must suspect that it can God take millions of years to just know about what is going on with his toes. Or perhaps God can travel a lot faster than light. And then, perhaps he can travel at such speed that millions of light-years become instantaneous. That would take a sort of infinite speed. Or perhaps God is out of space and time. But then how does he connect with space and time? If God is relevant to our physical universe, he must. But does that mean in some sense he becomes limited by it? Then he has trouble traveling? Or perhaps he is instantaneously everywhere. That would be closer to omnipotence. But then again, can we even dare think that we can reason about, or start understanding, a being that is instantaneously everywhere in this expanding universe of millions of galaxies?

And then, what about time? How old is God? Well, he cannot be old or have time limits. If time extends limitlessly, God has already enough time, from infinity, to experience everything, to go everywhere, to know everything. God cannot have a beginning or he would have an end – and, within infinity in time, he would had died already...

So much for reasoning about God. We just cannot get there with reason. And even our mystic experiences of God are not really about the God of everything. I had no experience of the God of countless galaxies, and to my knowledge nobody ever has. Perhaps our mystic experiences are about some lesser God "only" connected with our whole planet or solar system. Even such a being would be totally out of our "normal" cognitive abilities. And when we talk about it, we are not talking about God but only about our experience of him/it.

As I have explained, I was obliged to quit understanding God rationally long ago. Also, I came to believe that any experience of God is far from what our limited three-dimensional brain can process and from what our mind can grasp. We do have experiences that may be astounding. Many of us feel we have neither the words nor the concepts for them. And if we try to describe them in words, we must know that we are already dealing with some vague maps, not the territory. So, can I even say something about God? I can. But it will be about my understanding of him or of it. It will not be about my real experience but about the traces of it kept in my mind and my brain.

But then … I do have some experiences and they modify me slowly (and sometimes quickly). They show me possibilities, they hint at other worlds. They help me find a sense and know how and where to look for inner transformation. I would even say that during these experiences, some alchemy takes place. Years ago, I asked a Tibetan Master: "Why did I come back into being the same after my cosmic experience?" He just answered quietly: "You were not the same when you came back." And he was right. Sometimes if feels as if something far from words is "looking" at the world from my heart. And this "something" is full of love. It makes no distinction between nice or evil beings. It loves saints and demons alike. It feels no distance, it builds no barriers. I only feel a drop of the ocean of love and writing about this "ocean," which is also only a minor image for something I just cannot experience fully, brings me to tears. Paradoxically, saying that God is this or that is as relevant as saying God is not this or that. Perhaps we come closer in words by saying God is absolute "beingness" and "lovingness."

Do I love God? Another paradox: When I feel I love something, there is already some awareness about this thing or being I love. But I am not really aware of God as something I know. I am not aware, but still I feel awe and love towards something unknown.

And this brings me to another aspect. Perhaps it is not me, this little writer using a computer at this moment, who loves and feels God. Perhaps something in me is closer to him. I do know by experience that my soul is not this ego. I know my soul is already something venerable. It feels like a fountain of light and joyful love, a silent voice that always has wise words if and when I listen. Some words from Christ reverberate in my mind. Something like: "Through Me you go towards the Lord." The Christ was the supreme demonstration and incarnation of pure soul – again according to my own experiences and the writings from esoteric authors such as Alice Bailey (1965). So, I think He meant that we personal egos cannot go to God and meet Him but our souls can. I even believe that the cosmic consciousness experience I had was not me having it but my soul or even my inner individuality.

Still, I am following a spiritual path and I feel homesick. Or there is a deep sweet homesickness in me. Coming home is about feeling a permanent closeness to God. The God that lives in the more intimate of intimate places, the temple inside my heart. A flame is a good symbol for this and it feels like it is always there, emanating light and love and power.

In recent years, I noticed that my experiences with the Divine left me with the two traumas I mentioned before. Now, those are the traumas I am interested in working on. I feel indeed that the biographical drama of life is not so important to me. I want to go beyond Vitor, not to entertain myself with his shortcomings, fears, desires, frustrations, pains or triumphs. I did some work on Vitor but now I want more than him, even if I try to avoid the trap of believing I am perfect or I have no troubles. I may have some but I am no longer really interested unless I feel them as obstacles in my way to the Divine and to becoming a good channel of pure Love. I am a lot more interested in the Divine Presence and in opening my mind to a higher mind and my heart to a higher love.

If I want to be honest, I must acknowledge this instead of being afraid of what others will think or say about me. When I started working on this article and before I had a deep and moving experience of sharing emotional and spiritual experience with the fellow writers of this book, I would never have dreamt that I would assert this. But let us not be careful: aren't we in a quest for truth? So, this is my truth now.

How is this Relevant to Psychotherapy?

Let us come back to the "real" world. What about therapy? I am a psychologist and a psychotherapist. I know that modified states of consciousness can be extremely useful during psychotherapeutic sessions as they help clients find deeper and faster insights about themselves and powerful ways to reprogram their minds, emotions and bodies (Rodrigues & Friedman, 2013). I also know that sometimes "cosmic consciousness" or "samadhi" states (Weil, 1977a,b) can be real life-changers, but then again sometimes they are not enough.

I had one obsessive-compulsive client who went through an apparently typical cosmic state but then, after a few days, returned to his obsessive-compulsive patterns of thought and behavior. I had a cosmic consciousness experience but then I came back to being Vitor Rodrigues again, at least to some extent. So, even extremely powerful, deep, nice experiences may be not enough to dramatically change us. That part takes quite a lot of work – and indeed it is in a way signaled and facilitated by consciousness modification. Transpersonal consciousness-modifying tools such as meditation, breathwork, mantras, prayer, sacred dance and others become ways for opening new doors for self-understanding but also for self-modification. Leonard and Murphy (2005) call them "transformative practices." Sometimes, they even become ways for self-alchemy, qualitatively changing who we are. But then where is God in therapy? Is it in the therapist, in the client, in both? In the process? In the mysterious way some clients find their therapists or some therapists get their clients? Probably all of that, as all must belong in what some call God's ways.

I wish I could induce a deep, long-lasting feeling of inner sacredness of the Soul and inner Presence of the Divine in my clients. What would happen if I could induce that sense of solemnity and silence, which is the companion to a feeling of the inner sacred? I am sure that the majority of their psychological ailments would just vanish. Why? Because that would entail a radical change in their feeling of themselves.

Let me explain why as I explain something about stress (Rodrigues, 2013): it is a general "alert" reaction of the organism to threats *perceived* either internally or externally. That means it doesn't occur if nothing is perceived as a real threat (even if it can occur when something is erroneously considered to be such). This also implies that without *evaluation*, there can be no stress reaction. But evaluation of what? Of the potential of something to be dangerous to the organism/person. Then we notice that any evaluation is done against some measure. Nothing is "big" without the notion of a measuring system that allows us to also consider other things to be small or medium-sized as we compare them, say, to our own height.

Now we come to the core aspect of any evaluation conducive to stress: the self. To me, everything is a threat or not a threat according to the way I think and feel about who I am, my relevant aspects and my vulnerabilities. This is why, at a fundamental level, "saints" are a lot less vulnerable than regular humans to the stresses of life and to anything that can go against their bodies or their human personalities: they, as personalities, are not relevant to themselves as they identify with something else that is deeper and is Divine. That "thing" they identify with cannot be affected by the slings and arrows of outrageous fortune (to bring in something from Shakespeare) so they will not feel really threatened if they lose everything personal or if their physical life is threatened. They are in touch with the realms of the Divine immortal.

Even the impact of past memories, the traumatic ones, changes totally if I know that I am no longer the person who suffered past events. If my identity has changed, I am no longer that guy who was a victim or a perpetrator in the past: therefore, the effects of trauma no longer concern me. This is, in my view, the most powerful therapeutic possibility of all: a radical change in identity.

We find it also at least partially in people who had near-death experiences as the way they thought and felt about themselves changed through this powerful event in their lives, and as many lost the fear of death, their identity changed and situations that would normally be a big deal to them became harmless or just normal (according to Atwater, 2009).

For me, one of the biggest assets of transpersonal psychotherapy is that through the deep inner experiences and experiences of our environment it invites and promotes, we find new visions of who we are, what our life is all about, what our deeper layers may be and what different worlds are "out there" – or within the ocean of life. Such experiences do change our identity at a deep level and many times they don't just leave us powerful memories for different sensory perceptions and inner "adventures" in our distant past or other worlds of light and darkness; they don't just leave us with sometimes radically different perceptions about ourselves and the world we live in: they also entail a sort of "energy residue" that may amount to deeper powers for understanding life and acting in harmony with deep nature, society and the cosmos.

So, in a way, they may be extremely empowering while also detaching us from our usual, egotistic, mundane sense of "self." They give us impulses towards a different identity that consciously knows and feels an essential unity with everything that is. They change our ethics as we learn, through them, supreme values that are far away from consumerism, from the fear of loss connected with cravings and desires or from the fear of death.

Such values concern deep, satisfying-by-itself love that flows from within; awe about life, beauty and harmony; a sense of justice; a solemn respect for truth; or a need for wisdom. Perhaps we even sense, beyond all supreme values, a sense of the Divine. As we adopt them and act from them, we also find a sense of being in touch with, and at the service of, something higher than ourselves. According to Wallach (2009), this is the essence of spirituality. Visited by a sense of transcendence, we are no longer so shaken by mundane moments either of scarcity or abundance, fear or courage, pride or humbleness.

There is another aspect to this. When I am doing a session with a client, I try my best to stay in an open state of consciousness that goes along with a feeling of sacredness and solemnity both inside myself and the client. I know this may help the client, sometimes at an unconscious level, getting closer to the best he is and the best he can be: his higher self or soul. Perhaps therapists can be useful to their clients even without exchanging any words with them. I totally believe this. Let me explain what recently reinforced that belief.

A Little Experience with the Power of Prayer

I had a young boy, twelve years old, as a client. His parents brought him to me as he was exhibiting strange behavior, such as telling his teacher that he did not do the homework even when he had or always being negative, aggressive and destructive. So, in our first session, he told me that he would accept going through therapy and he would try to improve. At the next session, he told me that he really wanted to produce pain in his parents, that he was doing everything on purpose, that he had great joy in damaging people. He was happy that he had deceived me into believing he would collaborate. It seemed that I was talking to the "devil's seed" in person. I had a very strange feeling that something evil was emanating from this boy, something that I had never felt with such depth from a child.

I later called his parents into the room and had him confess that he loved the idea of impinging suffering on them. Then I told them that probably only medication would help and as he was not ready to cooperate in any sense I was charging nothing and "please call me back later." After this, I called a friend of mine, a very powerful clairvoyant, asking for her view about the boy. She told me that he was the prey of extremely dark forces and it was even a big danger to me having received him in my premises. She concluded that it was good that I wouldn't be working with him anymore. Indeed, I felt powerless to help so I prayed, asking the Divine to help to this boy.

A couple of weeks later, I received a phone call from his mother. She was extremely happy, thanking me for the deep improvement. She told me her boy was "back" to normal, behaving properly, a sweet, well-meaning young boy. I hadn't told her that I would pray for her child so she thought that in some mysterious way my two sessions had done the miracle. Months later, she called me again, still thanking me as the positive results were stable. I don't believe for a moment that what happened was due to my personal intervention. Something else moved there and got the boy free. I am sure it was due to the very positive and powerful forces from other layers of the universe.

"Dark Forces"?

This example brings us to something very strange. If I believe in God and I had some experiences that brought me a feeling of awe and sacredness, do I believe in the devil? Do I believe the world is the area where two big opposing invisible forces, Divine and devilish, are battling? No, I don't believe that and I don't feel it would make sense. I feel, from my inner experiences also, that there is a fundamental unity of the universe. However, I respect the notion that the "devil," meaning the "adversary," represents forces that go against unity: separation forces that stop us from being in touch with this unity. They may exist both in us and outside, coming from conscious beings who identify with separation.

In that sense, perhaps we do have devilish beings around (and sometimes we may be the little devils). Then, aside from "normal" reasons for psychological suffering and disturbances, perhaps some psychopathology can be due to the action of "invisible" beings acting against some people. I did have, many times in my sessions, clients describing such forces to me. And they described two sorts: regular humans who had died and for some reason either go against them on purpose or just hang around, producing some disturbance without really knowing it, and (rarely) some other beings that are interpreted as demons of some sort. Generally speaking, the clients who told me about such forces or entities were not psychotic, had relatively normal lives and jobs and could produce a distinction between themselves and their feelings and reality. They were not really paranoid about others and did not believe in Santa Claus or dragons. They could get suddenly surprised and very fearful during sessions. So, even without believing in a dual universe, I think that considering the possibility of strange, perhaps even dark forces mingling in our sessions, is not a bad idea. Then again, when clients are able to ask for help from deep within themselves, not out of anger or fear but preferably out of love, asking for Divine forces to remove whatever is hanging around them, they may get long-lasting positive effects.

Is this scientific? Not even close. Scientifically, we can say some clients describe this and get improvement in their situations when we work with them, considering with respect the possibility that they are not delusional. Of course, we are still not able to fully test, prove or discard in a scientific way the existence of God or the devil or just life after death, spirits and the like. However, we can find testimonies about them in spiritual traditions, esoteric schools and the individual experience of numerous, non-psychotic human beings (and of course also in psychotics, but then we could believe more easily that they are only producing the whole thing from deranged brains). Scientific discussions of relevant evidence for the life after death issue and the possibility of other worlds can be found in some recent work in parapsychology (Schmicker, 2002; Stevenson, 1997a,b; Tart, 2009; Van Lommel, 2006).

Now let me get back to something a lot more "psychological." Is there a psychological correspondence to what the spiritual traditions consider to be the core of "evil" and separation from "Divine realms"? Certainly. The Buddhists call it "negative emotions" and we are talking about aversions, fear, repulsion and rejection. Trauma leaves long-lasting negative emotions. The trouble is that aversions reinforce the ego structure as they reinforce the feeling of separation (and eventually loneliness) and the boundaries "outside" of us. When I go against anything in me or outside me, I produce separation and fracture.

Once again, the absolute opposite is on the side of numinous experiences and feelings of the Divine: they concern expansion of consciousness and the loss of "personal" boundaries. They feed on love that moves us towards something that we know goes far from our "human identities." They belong in the realms of unity. They contribute to very deep changes in the identity structure and opening to the limitless presence of something we call "God." In this sense, also, closeness to God (or the experience of something we have no words for but that feels radically "real" and truthful and good) is healing: it reduces or suppresses the fear of death, and it goes against feelings of loneliness, powerlessness or the lack of sense in life. No wonder scientific research, after reviewing hundreds of research projects, shows that religion (not fanaticism, of course) is healthy, brings better mental and physical health, improves resilience and reduces stress (Koenig, McCullough & Larson, 2001); good to know in a world where about five billion people, the vast majority of the human population, do have some spiritual or religious belief or adherence (Hitchcock & Esposito, 2004).

What else can I say? God is to me, increasingly, the supreme reference. If I am close to something indescribable that I would call the Divine, I feel a deep and silent venerable force in me. It moves me to being as harmless as I can and to love everything and every being. It produces a feeling of goodness and happy consciousness in the simplest actions. It brings peace of mind and even physiological peace. In the deepest sense, being separated from the Divine is now what I mostly avoid and coming home to "it" is what I strive for. To my knowledge, my clients benefit from this even when nothing is said about "it" and even when I do not try to "convert" them to anything. So, God be with us all.

References

Atwater, P. M. H. (2011). *Near-death experiences: The rest of the story.* Charlottesville, VA: Hampton Roads.

Atwater, P. M. H. (2008): Near-death states: the pattern of aftereffects. Paper presented at the First International Congress on Ecstatic States. Hannover Medical School, Germany, May.

Bailey, Alice A. (1965): *From Bethlehem to Calvary.* New York: Lucis Trust.

Hitchcock, S. T., & Esposito, J. L. (2004). *Geografia da religião* [Geography of religion]. Lisbon, Portugal: Lusomundo Editores.

Koenig, H. G., McCullough, M. E., & Larson, D. B. (2001). *Handbook of religion and health.* Oxford, UK: Oxford University Press.

Leonard, G. & Murphy, M. (2005). *The life we are given.* New York: Jeremy P. Tarcher/Penguin.
Rodrigues, V. & Friedman, H. (2013). Transpersonal psychotherapies, Ch. 32, *in* Friedman, Harris L. & Hartelius, G. (Eds.): *Handbook of transpersonal psychology.* West Sussex, England: Wiley-Blackwell.
Rodrigues, V. (2013). Tranquila-mente [Peacefully-minded]. Lisboa: Editora A Esfera dos Livros.
Rumi (2003). *The book of love.* New York: HarperCollins Publishers, Inc.
Schmicker, M. (2002). *Best evidence.* Lincoln, NE: iUniverse, Inc.
Stevenson, I. (1997 a and b). *Reincarnation and biology*: A contribution to the aetiology of birthmarks and birth defects. Volume 1: Birthmarks; and Volume 2: Birth defects and other anomalies. Westport CT: Praeger Publishers.
Tart, C. (2009). *The end of materialism.* Oakland, CA: New Harbinger Publications, Inc.
Van Lommel, P. (2006). *Conscience et cerveau. Actes du colloque "l'experience de mort imminente"* [Consciousness and the brain]. Proceedings from the Colloquium "The Near-Death Experience." Martigues: S17 Production.
Wallach, H. (2009). Spirituality: the legacy of parapsychology. *Archive for the Psychology of Religion, 31* (2009) 277-308.
Weil, P. (1993). Antologia do extase [Anthology of ecstasy]. São Paulo, SP: Editora Palas Athena9+
—. (1977a). A consciência cósmica [A cosmic consciousness]. Petrópolis: Editora Vozes Ltda.
—. (1977b). Análise de conteúdo de relatos obtidos em estado de consciência cósmica [Content analysis of accounts obtained in a cosmic consciousness state]. *Psicologia Clínica e Psicoterapia.* Belo Horizonte, *Interlivros, I (2):*55-82.

CHAPTER SIX

ARRIVING AT MYSELF, COMING HOME TO GOD

DIETRICH FRANKE

Abstract: In this contribution, two ways are shown through which coming back to oneself and towards God could be possible. While one way is characterized by a striving for mindful presence, the other need –above all – is to surrender into and trust God's guidance. Both ways are illustrated by personal experiences stemming from dreams and other states of extended consciousness as well as texts from different mystical traditions like the poem "The way home" from John of the Cross.

Keywords: dreams, mindful presence, mystical poems, states of extended consciousness, trust into God's guidance

Foreword

I am aware of how privileged I am as I write down my thoughts on the topic of "Coming Home," allowing me to explore my inner home. I am grateful to have a safe, stable outer home with a roof over my head and to live in a nice area. It is warm, I have enough to eat, I have a loving wife by my side and I am part of a stable social network. It is far less comfortable for people who have to leave their home, don't have one or are unable to return home because they are on the run, homeless or are asylum seekers living in conditions of extreme deprivation in a foreign country. I extend my sympathy to all of these people.

I will be discussing two aspects of homecoming in close detail: first "arriving within myself through a mindful presence" followed by "coming home to God." In this exploration, I would also like to describe some very personal experiences of mine. In the words of Carl Rogers – the father of humanistic psychology – “what is most personal is most general.”[1] Rogers believed that our most private and personal experiences resonated the most with other people, if only we were willing to share.

Arriving at Myself through a Mindful Presence

An hour ago, I returned from Switzerland by car and I am now sitting on a chair in my garden with a laptop in front of me, writing these words. It is a typical day in early spring; the sun is shining in a blue sky and I feel the warmth of it on my face… I have just mowed the lawn and I can smell the scent of freshly cut grass… I can hear the birds chirping on the roof… I raise my eyes and I can see the green lawn in my neighbors’ garden, where I notice the bright yellow of the forsythias and underneath them lies a small pile of cut branches and brown leaves… I can feel the soft breeze on my skin, now it is a little stronger, then it grows weaker… the noise of a plane flying overhead reaches my ears… the noise of the airplane’s turbines comes closer and I feel myself growing annoyed at this disturbance… then the noise slowly ebbs away along with my anger… my thoughts wander to the past few days, which I spent in a Benedictine monastery in Switzerland, in the circle of all of my colleagues from the Institute. We spent three days presenting and discussing our contributions to the book, and I feel deep gratitude for this gathering. The faces of all my friends appear before my inner eye and a warm feeling washes over me… I spend a few moments with this feeling in my chest and allow it to reside in me… I take in the stillness… after a while, I decide to direct my attention to my feet (the soles of my feet are my preferred point of anchoring during meditation when my spirit has gone wandering). I can feel a light tickling sensation there… it is as if my feet are happy that I am paying attention to them… now I feel the urge to take a bite out of the apple that is lying on the table… I decide to stop writing and give in to the urge, granting myself a little break so I can eat the apple in peace… while I do this, I notice three storks in the sky and I follow them with my gaze as they fly above me in circles… I feel joy as I watch them and I feel my chest opening up and my breathing becoming deeper… I feel a deep peace, I feel safe and satisfied with life and all of its expressions.

When I manage to be mindful in the way I have just described, and I am able to simply shift my attention to the present moment instead of

---

[1] Rogers, C. quoted in Marti, L. (2013, p. 12), see reference list.

always thinking of the future, it seems as though I have finally arrived IN myself, that I have become more and more at one with the world, and I am in harmony with everything that is – even with my passing anger over the airplane noise. For one (most often short) moment, I can rest in this joyful way and I often long to be in it more often. It actually sounds quite simple and yet my experience tells me that I have to keep learning to do this from scratch, always learning to be mindful of being present in the moment. This constant practice of being-in-the-moment has become vital for me to lead a fulfilled life and for my psychotherapeutic work. Even though the term mindfulness is well known today, and a great number of books and articles have been written regarding this topic, I would like to go into the subject even more thoroughly at this point.

So, what do I need in order to anchor my attention to the here and now? First of all, I need to have the intention of doing exactly that. Why do I then often find it difficult to be present in a mindful way? It is, above all, my preconceptions, judgments, aversions and preferences that – often unnoticed by myself – distract my attention away from the current moment and divert it somewhere else, most often into the future or the past. Now, if I want to practice becoming more alert in the present, I have to first be aware of these distractions. For example, when I unconsciously wish to be somewhere else than in this moment right now, I have to catch myself so that I can re-establish a mindful presence in this moment, and I can re-center my attention. Of course, I know that my mind, by nature, has a strong tendency to wander. This knowledge can also be consoling. I don't have to worry about this evolutionary tic that causes our minds to constantly be alert in order to notice any possible dangers. I can be thankful for this guardian-like function. It means I can calmly and complacently accept that I will always inevitably fail in my attempts to anchor my mind in the here and now. Despite this insight, should my inner critic attempt to bother me, then I will simply respond to it with the attitude, "Isn't it good that I have noticed that my attention has wandered, because now I am present once again!"

I would like to illustrate the subject of mindfulness with a simple model (I like simple models): The "Wheel of Consciousness" (Siegel, 2012, p. 144). Imagine that mindfulness is the wheel of a bicycle. The hub is at the center of the wheel. It is connected to the outer edge (the rim) with spokes. This wheel demonstrates everything that our attention can be focused on: thoughts, feelings, bodily sensations or events in the external world. The spokes represent how our attention is focused on a specific part of the edge.

Our attention is conditioned to concentrate on familiar, comfortable experiences and avoid unfamiliar ones. The hub represents the place in our mind where we are conscious of all that we perceive. Our awareness rests in the hub while we focus our attention on different things just as the spokes point to different parts of the rim of the wheel. Out of habit, our attention leaves the hub and moves along the spokes and attaches itself in turn to different parts of the rim (such as plans, wishes, evaluations, unfinished business, fears, etc.) or it can get lost in endless trains of thought and narratives. While our attention will naturally gravitate in and out of the moment, it will continually hook on to something on the edge of our experience. So, if I feel bound to the hub and my attention gets caught in the rim, I become separated from my wholeness, I do not really feel at home in myself, I find myself in a kind of trance.

Mindfulness training has taught me to lead my attention back to the hub after it has wandered away and to anchor it there; then I can connect again to the reality of the here and now. This anchor can help to calm my mind. In this way, mindfulness can provide the path to lead me to the home inside myself. Mindfulness helps us to take things as they come with serenity and to see their nature clearly. If, despite this, I find judgmental and negative opinions inside me, I accept this and do not blame myself for them. Instead, I adopt a friendly, empathetic and loving attitude towards myself. Developing and caring for such a loving feeling towards yourself is, to me, the central part of every mindfulness practice. It allows me to view myself in a softer and more caring way and makes my inner, more critical voice fade a little more.

If I want to arrive fully at myself, in my true Self, my essence, then I have to firstly – and this might be painful – push away my familiar self-identity, let go of my internalized parents and the rules and limitations I absorbed from them. This will at first cause fear because I won't know what to expect next. I have been holding on to my self-identity because it has given me a feeling of safety – but when it dissolves, it may feel like a kind of death. I have to first learn that the true Self can only unfold if I accept the emptiness and the connected state of unknowing and lie in it in mindful peace. I find that in this state of unknowing, stillness and space flow from it and lead to feelings of benevolence and joy.

Arriving within myself and coming home to my true being mean an acceptance of my whole reality as it is. They also mean acceptance of those things that I am most reluctant to see: old pain, inconvenient truths about myself, unloved characteristics, my disasters, my failures – by making peace with and accepting my darker side, I come ever closer to becoming a whole person. We often spend a lot of time and energy trying to reach a certain goal. Even when traveling down a specific path in life is out of the question, it seems equally important to recognize that a focus on the future can lead to an endless race and can be very stressful. We always feel we have to achieve more in order to feel sufficiently worthy. I allow myself to stop from time to time and grant myself a "sacred pause" (Brach, 2012) so I can allow myself to connect with the realm of a natural presence. Perhaps I can sense the stillness and emptiness, and recognize that I have already arrived in this place and in this moment, I have, at this very second, already crossed the finish line. If I let myself fall into this feeling of already having arrived, I can then receive peace, contentment and joy. By saying quietly to myself: "I'm there… I'm there… I'm there…" and letting the flow of my breath and my attention synchronize, and feeling my way mindfully into my body, I can be aware that I have arrived in a wholly complete moment. Even if this moment still contains far-off goals or unsatisfied needs, it is as if I have arrived on the other side of the river, and it has opened up new experiences. If I can manage not to try and control my momentary experiences, regardless of their form, I can be free from my expectation of what these experiences should be. I can stop fighting against uncomfortable experiences or letting myself be judged by their presence. Through this, I can find a natural, mindful peace. Then, even if it is just for a short moment, I have arrived home.

At this point, I would like to recount a personal experience that has shaped my whole life as well as the way I approach my work as a psychotherapist and I deal with my clients. This experience happened 30 years ago. Back then, I was traveling widely through the Brazilian Amazon region in South America, and I had the opportunity to take part in an *ayahuasca* ritual. The term 'ayahuasca' comes from the Inca language and can be loosely translated as 'the vine of the spirits.' It is a psychedelic substance widely used among the indigenous tribes in the Amazon. Produced from a vine and a leafy plant, it is used in ritualistic practice – in a carefully controlled environment – as a healing substance for physical and psychological illnesses, for the manifestation of visions and as a sacrament in a spiritual context. Up to that point, I had never had any experiences with psychedelic substances but since my youth, I had always had an inexplicable affinity to South American culture, especially the Amazon. A deep desire led me to travel to Brazil with my wife. In my bag, I had packed a novel called *Wizard of the Upper Amazon* (Lamb, 1985). It is based on facts and describes the initiation of a young white man, who is kidnapped by an indigenous tribe. He later rises to become the chieftain of their tribe. In the many steps of the initiation in which he takes the place of the old chieftain, the ritual use of ayahuasca plays an important role. What

I only found out later was that this narrative took place in the exact same region in which I had my ayahuasca experience. It was one of many strange coincidences that I experienced during my journey. I have since learned to play close attention to any kind of coincidence that arises in my life. But now to the initiation itself. An extract from the recollection I wrote the next day may give you an impression of what occurred:

"I experience a cascade of playful shapes that flow and melt into each other and are of a blue-green color. These shapes are not compact, but have a very fine and subtle quality. Everything is moving – nothing is still. From time to time, it seems to me as if a veil has been lifted, as if the truth will reveal itself to me, and it will arise from the depths of my everyday consciousness where it has been buried, as if it will reveal to me what it is that holds the world together at its very core. Everything seems to be interconnected, there are no divisions and no opposites, no good or evil, no better or worse, everything is equal. Everything – even the matter – is alive, has a consciousness. I spend some time being in touch with a tree, which I perceive to be a living being. I experience a deep connection and I let myself be deeply touched by beauty and perfection. I feel the same deep experience of connection and love with the people around me, as I have never felt them before. I am simply amazed in the face of all of this wonder. I experience an unbound joy as well as a deep respect for everything that is living and its inner intelligence. I feel a deep gratitude. I cry out of sheer happiness. For a moment, it seems as if all the mysteries and secrets will reveal themselves to me. I am standing in front of a kind of gate and I feel certain: if I open this door, I will encounter God. Yet I cannot open this door, and what lies behind it remains a secret (since this experience, I have always referred to God as the 'great secret' or 'mystery'). It becomes clear to me that I cannot facilitate an encounter with God by myself, but that a complete devotion, released from all aspirations to my ego, is possible through God's mercy, and I may feel his presence. But – I can't do it alone."

I had prepared paper and pencils for my journey in order to immediately note down any realizations. The attempt to shape the essence of my experience into words was confounded, however, and often ended in great bouts of laughter. Our language seemed far too coarse, and my attempt to describe the essence and details of what I had experienced in words seemed ridiculous. Therefore, a lot of what I experienced on my journey into the previously unknown and unexplored parts of my soul will stay unspoken.

Perhaps the language of poetry is better suited to gaining closer access to the mysteries of life, as in von Eichendorff's[2] poem "Wünschelrute" [Divining rod] from 1835:

> A song sleeps in all things
> Which dream on and on,
> And the world begins to sing,
> If only you find the magic word.

The essence of my experience has of course shaped and sparked a transformation in me, which is still potent in some mysterious way. And what I could not have suspected then is that this strange experience would later prove to show me what I would now describe as being an essential part of my self-image: making it possible for people to go on their shamanic journeys, accompanying them in their experience and supporting them as they integrate what they have sensed and experienced. During the trip to the Swiss Benedictine monastery with my colleagues, I was abruptly awoken by a dream during my second night there. It brought to my mind that the ayahuasca experience in the Brazilian rainforest was just one part of my spiritual journey to meet God and become a whole person.

I am wide awake, as if electrified. Before I can consider a possible interpretation of my dream, I realize with a start that twenty-five years ago, I had awoken out of a dream just as suddenly as I had now. The memory of this old dream pushes itself to the forefront of my mind, and the next day, I meditate on what the possible meanings could be. I will come back to the newer dream later.

Twenty-five years ago, I was taking part in a two-day workshop on the topic "Dreamwork with Focusing," led by Gene Gendlin, a student and colleague of Carl Rogers, and the founder of the focusing approach in psychotherapy (Gendlin, 1981). I had packed the manuscript of my dissertation on *Focusing in the context of the theory of the two hemispheres of the cerebrum* (Franke, 1985), which I was planning to give to Gendlin. I had written this dissertation two years before but then fell into a deep depression and did not manage to take the necessary steps to finish my degree and graduate. This depression lasted until the time of this workshop. But now, back to my dream:

I am on my way to the second day of the workshop. I am desperate to tell the other participant that I have only just been released from the hospital, where they successfully operated on a ten-centimeter-long wound

---

[2] Joseph Freiherr von Eichendorff (1788 – 1857), German Romantic lyric poet and writer.

on my heart. The group room is full of noise, but Gendlin gives me a microphone so that I can tell the group about my dream without having to raise my voice.

The next day, I tell the group of my dream at the beginning of the workshop – exactly as I did in the dream but this time I can make myself heard without a microphone. The meaning of my dream seemed clear as day to me and needed no further interpretive work. When I handed my manuscript to Gene Gendlin at the end of the workshop, I felt a sense of relief, a feeling of happiness and freedom. My depression seemed to end quite suddenly, and was later followed by a euphoric upswing and an intense surge of energy that enabled me to hand in my dissertation and take all the steps to gain my doctorate.

In close connection to the dream I have just described is another dream that marked the beginning of the dark night of my soul two years previously. At that time, my wife Beatrix was in her fifth month of pregnancy. We were both taking part in a focusing conference, in which I had signed up for a workshop on dreamwork with focusing. This dream was in two parts. In the first part, I dreamed:

I am lying on my back on the floor and I hold my newborn child into the air. We both beam and smile at each other and I am happy and full of joy...

Then the dream turns dark – I am in a cemetery, the details of which I cannot remember exactly. I only know that the mood is dark, oppressive and very scary.

Today, twenty-seven years later, I am still fascinated by the precision with which my soul had visualized my emotional state at the time and the two great themes that it mirrored: life and death. The dream I had had at the beginning of my depression did not simply point towards the upcoming birth of our daughter but also made the newborn's symbolization of life, vitality and rebirth visceral for me so that I could actually feel it. The second part of the dream pointed towards the theme of dying and death and announced my upcoming depression. The fact that I cannot remember any exact details from this part of the dream may mean that I was simply not ready at the time to let myself explore this horrifying topic more deeply.

My depression began about a half year after my return from the South America journey during which I had the ayahuasca experience. I remember my "darkness of the soul" as being very painful and sorrowful. Even though I wished then for nothing more than for this torture to be over, I knew without a doubt that I did not want to resort to antidepressants. I could not give a reason for this decision, it came out of an intuitive urge, out of rational knowledge. It seemed to me unavoidable that I had to cross this deep and dark valley and that I had to bear this oppressive heaviness of depression without any shortcuts or allowing myself chemically-induced relief. I did not and could not do anything about it, I simply wanted to learn to trust that I could eventually, at a time completely out of my control, come out of the darkness of the underworld and back into the light of day. But it was certainly not easy to learn how to trust. I remember vividly how I fell into a deep despair, plagued by suicidal thoughts as I stood in front of the locked door of the local church at night, saying out loud to myself the first lines of a hymn: "From deep affliction I cry out to you, Lord God, hear my call." But I did not hear an answer from God – perhaps I had missed one of his signs – until one day, this dream was sent to me, ringing in the end of my depression.

Before I begin to describe what meaning I can retrospectively give to my depression and in what way it granted me greater access to God, I would like to outline a thought. If, twenty-five years ago, I had already had the command over the mindfulness practice that I have today, or had I had access to the broad literature on mindfulness and self-empathy that is available now, I might have found a preventative or a way of dealing with my depression, such as in the following model that I will quickly describe now. It is the RAIN model.

The word RAIN (Brach 2012, p. 40) is an acronym, composed of the first letters of the following steps:

R: Recognize what is happening
A: Allow life to be just as it is
I: Investigate with kindness
N: Non-identification

Recognize and name what is happening in this moment: I may ask myself: "Is there sadness? Anger? Fear?

Allow life to be just as it is: I can allow all of my experiences (thoughts, feelings and sensations) to be just as they are.

Investigate with kindness: I can ask myself in a kind and loving way, "How am I feeling everything that is happening inside my body (e.g. my pain and suffering)? Do my sensations stay the same or do they change over time?"

Non-identification: I view my current suffering as a kind of energy that is visiting me. I do not see it as something unique to myself but as something that I share with a lot of other people – just like raindrops (RAIN) that fall on every human being equally.

The RAIN process can help me ward off difficult emotions so I do not lose myself in them. Through this, I can see that these emotions – just like all other things in life – can change. They arise and then they pass again so I don't have to be afraid of being trapped in them forever.

There is another quality that lies close to my heart because it brings lightness into my life, and in difficult times it gives me a sense of the "cosmic game" or the feeling of being in "God's comedy." In especially painful states, it is a very important resource – it is humor. As Falkenberg et al. (2013) have shown, a sense of humor can, like other aspects of oneself, be learned through training so not only can psychiatric and psychosomatic patients benefit from it but also their therapists.

Humor can be described as the "ability of a person to meet with serenity the inadequacy of people and of the world, the difficulties and the frustration of the everyday" (Ruch, 2012).

Metzner (2013) describes **HUMOR** as an inner attitude, which, parallel to the characteristics of mindfulness, is marked by the following qualities:

- **H-** Kindness of the **H**eart
- **U-** **U**nderstanding the incongruous and absurd
- **M-** **M**ustering courage
- **O-** **O**penness
- **R-** **R**elativizing your own opinions and judgments

Since humor, in comparison to cynicism and sarcasm, is not based on mean-spiritedness or *Schadenfreude* but is instead the expression of genuine friendliness and interest, kindness of the **Heart** or loving goodness (metta) is part of a humorous attitude. In Buddhism, kindness of the heart is a part of compassion (karuna), empathetic joy (mudita) and equanimity (upekka), all of which form the "four immeasurables" (Thich Nhat Hanh, 2016).

A humorous attitude helps us to **understand** the absurdities, incongruities and paradoxes of life as well as helps us to meet the limitations of our own beliefs with serenity. They are not necessarily dissolved through this approach but can, in my opinion, be more easily accepted with a laugh and a smile. "Through laughter we can allow contradictions to stand without having to destroy them. Our reason wants to organize the world but it is far too complex to divide what is good/evil, right/left, true/false" (Hirschhausen, 2012: 291).

It is necessary to **muster courage** because it allows humor to actively and constructively change our world of experience, despite adverse conditions, and enable a change of perspective.

Openness means, on the one hand, that we can be open to a humorous situation and recognize our faults and weaknesses that we usually keep hidden. On the other hand, it also enables an open attitude towards other points of view, instead of stubbornly holding on to our views and insisting that ours is the only point of view. It is only when we let go that we become free to receive something new.

If we manage to **relativize** humor with our own concepts and attitudes, we can create an inner distance that can aid a different point of view and a change in perspective, which makes the painful side of life easier for us to bear.

Humor and mindfulness are related: while humor without mindfulness can manifest itself as biting cynicism and sarcasm, a serious and intense practice of mindfulness contains the danger that our efforts will take on a kind of grim quality of "spiritual athleticism." Mindfulness should therefore have a dash of "mindfoolness." Think of the fact that court jesters in medieval times and today during *Fastnacht* celebrations hold mirrors up to the faces of their targets and are allowed to speak uncomfortable truths without being punished. In this way, they give us insight into new perspectives and different possibilities of development.

I will now return to describing my phase of depression. As I look back, I think I understand that this experience of the dark night of my soul was necessary for the developmental path of my career and my spirituality, although the deeper meaning of my depression did not come to me until much later. On the surface level, I understood that I had to learn what it meant to suffer, and I had to practice humility and devotion. This experience of suffering taught me a strong sense of compassion for myself and for other people. This was a great benefit for my psychotherapeutic work with people suffering from depression because I could not only understand what they were going through but I could also feel it. I am absolutely certain that an important aspect of the healing process in the relationship between psychotherapist and patient is that they know the therapist can feel what they feel.

On another level, which I believe I can now understand better, I have come to reach the conclusion that my depression was vital for my spiritual development, because of the above-described experience of coming closer to God than ever before, and the way He saw into my darker side. I had to better understand the other side – the world of shadows – in order to learn that both sides belong together to build a unity. It is only when I accept this truth that the two complementing aspects of Dark and Light form a whole that I can allow myself to come home to myself and to God.

The Spanish mystic John of the Cross[3] points to this in his poem (Repges 1985: 115) *I Came Into the Unknown* when he states, "It is the *shadowy* cloud that clarified the night."

Coming Home to God

In this poem, John of the Cross describes the path of experience as a mystic, which is essentially the path to his meeting with God. It is not only my own experiences that I see mirrored in John's poem; I believe that all of us searching for spirituality will find validation in his narrative, and I would like to introduce this poem to you and give you my thoughts on it. This poem always releases in me a great inner resonance and I have often used it in my own meditation practice as well as with other people in their experiences of enhanced consciousness, such as shamanic rituals.

I Came Into the Unknown

I came into the unknown
and stayed there unknowing
rising beyond all science.

I did not know the door
but when I found the way,
unknowing where I was,
I learned enormous things,
but what I felt I cannot say,
for I remained unknowing,
rising beyond all science.

It was the perfect realm
of holiness and peace.
In deepest solitude
I found the narrow way:
a secret giving such release
that I was stunned and stammering,
rising beyond all science.

[3] John of the Cross (1542-1591), a Spanish mystic.

I was so far inside,
so dazed and far away
my senses were released
from feelings of my own.
My mind had found a surer way:
a knowledge of unknowing,
rising beyond all science.

And he who does arrive
collapses as in sleep,
for all he knew before
now seems a lowly thing,
and so his knowledge grows so deep
that he remains unknowing,
rising beyond all science.

The higher he ascends
the darker is the wood;
it is the shadowy cloud
that clarified the night,
and so the one who understood
remains always unknowing,
rising beyond all science.

This knowledge by unknowing
is such a soaring force
that scholars argue long
but never leave the ground.
Their knowledge always fails the source:
To understand unknowing,
rising beyond all science.

This knowledge is supreme
crossing a blazing height;
through formal reason tries
it crumbles in the dark,
but one who would control the night
by knowledge of unknowing
will rise beyond all science.

And if you wish to hear:
the highest science leads
to an ecstatic feeling
of the most holy Being;
and from his mercy comes his deed:
to let us stay unknowing,
rising beyond all science.

In this poem, John of the Cross is describing his path to an experience of God. Because he has been granted entry under extraordinary circumstances to a special realm of consciousness, it is possible for him to come home and encounter God. What he has experienced, as his narrative tells us, lies beyond our understanding and he cannot put it into words. Every attempt to put his experience into words leads him to stumble.[4]

Through an experience of an encounter with God, the mind has been gifted with something unspeakably large, beyond all knowledge, and which reaches beyond all intellectual understanding: it reaches a safe space that it can call home, and it gives a feeling of being safe and secure that is beyond all of our expectations of our impetus for safety, spurned by our controlling reason. We feel a sense of being looked after, which satiates our desires to feel accepted and secure. This kind of experience is only possible by letting yourself go.

That space in which you will find security and peace cannot be located and cannot be made concrete. Nor is it based on rational arguments or hard and fast concepts.

In Christianity, one speaks of the Heavenly Father, and yet no one can say for sure where heaven is – it exists outside of time and space. God is everywhere and nowhere, he is a kind of "I-don't-know-what"; he cannot be found and he cannot be seen objectively. I do not know where or what or who he is.

What else can you say about God, then?

It is only when we let ourselves go completely and devote ourselves fully that we can have an inkling of God and feel a part of him: his goodness, warm-heartedness, his mercy, everything that God exudes, his acceptance and his love for us. This is the goal of our spiritual path.

So how do I reach this goal? Next to the path of No, which means saying no to everything that God is not, John points to the path of Yes, which is marked by acceptance, devotion and love.

To encounter God, I have to empty myself of all expectations, images and concepts, let go of all philosophical systems and evidence for God, enter the "cloud of unknowing"[5] and the "cloud of forgetting" and "remain in a state of not understanding." Only then will my soul gain entrance to the realm that Jesus calls the Kingdom of Heaven.

Saying **Yes** to God means rising above all knowledge, and John of the Cross continually emphasizes this in his poem. So how do I say yes to

---

[4] Please compare this to my experience with ayahuasca.

[5] "The Cloud of Unknowing" is a text about a mystical path, written by anonymous author, England ca. 1390.

God? How do I transcend my knowledge? How do I find the one who is beyond all knowledge? John's answer to this is: God is love. But how can I find God's love? I find his love by believing in it. I believe in his love by:

- accepting it
- giving in to it
- returning it

Acceptance:

How can I accept God when my senses cannot perceive him and my reason cannot think about him?

Here, John of the Cross presents a paradox, an encouraging hint, almost like a koan[6]: It is the dark cloud that brightens the night.

How can we understand this?

Every night can be divided into three phases:

- dusk, in which everything that can be perceived slowly begins to disappear from sight
- midnight, the darkest period
- dawn, in which the light of a new day begins to shine.

These three phases help us picture the path a person may take to God: first, you must let all of your connections to worldly objects and your identification with the environment sink away – just as the growing dusk limits daylight. Our way to God is beyond all interpretation and an understanding of it is as dark as the middle of the night. Our goal – God – seems so different and strange, just as day is to night, and as strange as the dawn of morning to the darkest night. The night must admit defeat and make way for the light.

In this way, the dark night can also be the brightest light. When we suffer, God is near us. When we don't know what to do anymore, we are at our goal. When we feel weak, we are strong. The darker the night that surrounds us, the more hidden the meaning, the more hopeless the situation seems, the closer God is to us.

How can we understand this?

---

[6] In Zen Buddhism, a koan is a short aphorism given by a Master that at first seems to be paradoxical, incomprehensible and pointless.

To transcend the hopelessness of life and the connected feeling of helpless and impotence, finding God through all of this requires an acceptance of the hopelessness and our impotence.

That God is hidden in the darkest cloud can mean that this dark cloud can shine a light on our lives by bringing Him closer to us.[7]

In the deep disappointments of our lives, in the face of our mortality, in the night of our senses and of our mind, we can experience God and his mercy – depending on whether we accept our painful experiences and these so-called strokes of fate as challenges through which we can grow and understand.

Devotion:

God comes to us in the dark of the night. Accepting God means accepting his seclusion. To accept the darkness in which God shrouds himself and in which I can feel him and guess that he is there, I have to be prepared to let myself go. Accepting God also requires that I submit to him, trustingly. Especially when I don't know where else to go, when good counsel is scarce or not even available, when nothing is in sight, when my situation seems completely hopeless, when I feel helpless and impotent,[8] that is exactly when I have to devote myself and let myself fall into the unknown and the uncertainty. Then the rule applies: I'm not in charge anymore, you are. I will no longer decide, but you will. I will stop wrestling for control, trusting that I will "fall no further than into God's palm."[9]

Over the years, I learned that it was much more useful for the therapeutic process to simply be patient in times of not knowing what to do and accepting the feelings of tension, uncertainty and helplessness they

---

[7] John of the Cross experienced this in 1577 when opponents to his Reform captured him, abused him in a windowless dungeon and almost let him starve to death. In his abandonment in this dark prison, he had an encounter with God.

[8] This is a familiar situation in my work as a psychotherapist. I sometimes feel helpless and faint—when I see myself at a dead end, when none of my interventions help the person in front of me and I simply don't know what to do. If I find the courage to tell the other person about my helplessness and impotence (sharing this with my client) by saying, "I don't know what to do either. Now there are two helpless people sitting across from each other. We have that in common," it may happen – usually after a quite long silence – that something unfreezes and begins to flow again. A funny comment can also be good sometimes – depending on the situation – to bring back the flow.

[9] These are the words of former German Bishop Margot Käsmann, after she was caught drunk-driving by a police patrol. Shortly after, she resigned from all her posts.

brought with them. It was not something you could get rid of by doing something. I had to hope and trust that eventually a greater power than myself or the person in front of me would intervene and begin the healing process.

Those who dare to leap into the unknown[10] embark on the greatest journey of discovery known to man, according to John of the Cross. It is a journey full of adventure through the unknown, through undiscovered landscapes with a myriad of surprises for which no one can ever be prepared. We are rewarded for our courage and our trust through "the greatest conquest there can be." This conquest takes place in our heart: to conquer is to receive the love of God.

Love:

Love is the universal truth that penetrates everything, and being united in love with God is our deepest desire and ultimate goal. Whether I will reach this goal or not does not lie within my power, but is dependent on God's mercy, God's grace and God's goodness. Ultimately, everything merciful is the expression of God's unconditional love – especially in the dark night, in the unfulfilled, in my defeats, and setbacks and my failures. Through the connection to God's love, we may draw the strength and the confidence to go through life despite our suffering and our defeats.

Please compare these considerations to the words of the following poem, found in a collection of mystical texts from East and West (Jäger, W. and Grimm, B. 2010: 107)

God speaks

"When you come steadily nearer
And you do so with the fullest devotion,
Until you are at one with my love,
Then I am the ear with which you hear,
The eye through which you see,
The hand with which you feel,
The foot with which you walk."

I feel that this description of a connection to God's love has parallels to the observations of John of the Cross on the concept of saying Yes, and I

---

[10] John of the Cross dared to leap into the unknown during his escape from the dungeon. "And one night – it was August 1578 – he set his plan in motion. He had torn his bed sheets into strips and had tied them to each other. He tied the newly made rope to the crossed window bars and let himself descend on it. The rope was not long enough. John had to jump…" (Repges, W. 1985: 17).

would like to illustrate this with a personal experience from my younger self.

During a ritual including the consumption of psychedelic substances that was carefully led by two very experienced colleagues, I had an encounter with God, in which He appeared to me as a kind of fatherly friend. In this vision, a godly voice led me to see everything that was happening within me as well as outside of me. "Yes, this is exactly what is it like at this moment," he seemed to say. I understood his message as I could give everything a reason, I could acknowledge the existence of everything and I could trust in and respect the transformative power of acceptance instead of allowing myself to be caught in the useless and energy-draining struggle of setting myself against things. Finally, I began to understand that it was all about accepting everything with love – even my resistance, my reluctance, my desire to say No. This is the kind of love that is all-encompassing and that does not exclude anything. However, this does not mean saying "Yes and Amen" to everything that I encounter in life. Of course, it involves saying "Yes to everything that is," even, for example, the right to be angry about everything that is wrong in the world and to work towards fixing it.

I would now like to tell you of the dream I had while I was with my colleagues at the Swiss monastery, and I would like to give some thoughts on it.

I find myself with my second wife Annette at the edge of a river or a canal. It is cold and we are both dressed for winter weather. To my surprise, Annette goes towards the slightly raised muddy edge and begins to slip – the ground is slick – and as she can no longer keep her balance, she falls into the water and goes under. Because I know how good a swimmer she is, I wait a little bit in the hope that she will pop out of the water at any moment. But when only a few bubbles of air reach the surface, it becomes clear to me that I must jump into the water to find Annette. I am not panicked as I allow myself to glide into the water, and I even remember to leave my glasses on the riverbank. As I search for her underwater, I have the sinking realization that there is no hope of finding Annette in the dark and muddied water. In that moment, I wake up.

My dream contains an important message for my personal and spiritual path of development. I understand this sign to mean the following: it is my task to find the most important thing I possess in the depths (of my unconscious, my realm of emotions, my spirituality) and to bring it to the surface. I have to find a treasure, which obviously has feminine qualities and which not only points to my own *anima* but also to a godly aspect (underneath our rooms in the monastery, there was a grotto devoted to the

Virgin Mary). I cannot recognize anything in the depths because the water is murky and muddy. A pair of glasses – the usual method of seeing more clearly – cannot help me any further and I leave them on the riverbank. I am reminded of the "dark cloud" described by John of the Cross in his poem. This dream is obviously about a different kind of seeing, not with my eyes but in the sense of seeing with the heart. The ending of the dream remains open. So, I remain in the cloud of unknowing and I let my dream continue to bear upon me, trusting that the meaning will become clearer and tell me which step I should take next.

Afterword

A short while ago, I spent some time with a very dear and very ill friend, who is dealing with a metastasized tumor. She taught me what mindful presence truly means. It is uncertain how much time she has left to live – it could be months, weeks or even just days. It made a huge impression on me and touched me deeply to see how composed my friend is in the face of her mortality – being so anchored by her Christian belief. She has settled everything there is to settle: she has organized her entire estate. Barring a few essential objects, she has gifted or sold all of her furniture, books and other various items, and she had discussed her wishes for the burial and the funeral with the undertaker and the priest. She appeared to me as if she had been released, and was able to savor every moment of our being together with her mindful presence. She was deeply grateful for our relationship and prized all the small ordinary occurrences of life. She was ready to take the last journey home to another dimension, a dimension that lies beyond all our human knowledge.

References

Barnstone, W. (1999). *To touch the sky: Poems of mystical, spiritual and metaphysical light.* New York: New Directions Publishing Corporation. Retrieved on April 28, 2017 from www.poetry-chaikhana.com/blog/2013/08/05/john-of-the-cross-i-came-into-the-unknown-2/

Brach, T. (2012): Mindful presence. A foundation for compassion and wisdom. In C. Germer & R. Siegel (Eds.), *Wisdom and compassion in psychotherapy* (p. 35-47). New York (NY): Guilford Press.

Eichendorff, J.v. (1962): *Gesammelte Werke Bd. 1* [Collected works, Vol. 1] Berlin: Aufbau-Verlag.

Falkenberg, I., McGhee., P., & Wild, B. (2013): *Humorfertigkeiten Trainieren.Manual für die psychiatrisch-psychotherapeutische Praxis*

[Exercising humor skills. Manual for the psychiatric-psychotherapeutic practice] Stuttgart: Schattauer.

Franke, D. (1985): *Auf dem Weg zu einer ganzheitlichen Psychotherapie: Gendlin's Focusing auf dem Hintergrund der Hemisphärentheorie* [On the way to a holistic psychotherapy: E.T. Gendlin's Focusing in the context of the theory of the two hemispheres of the cerebrum]. Unveröffentlichte Dissertation [Unpublished doctoral dissertation].

Gendlin, E. (1981): *Focusing. Technik der Selbsthilfe bei der Lösung persönlicher Probleme* [Focusing. Technique of self-help to help solve personal problems]. Salzburg: Müller.

Hirschhausen, E. (2012): Humor hilft heilen. Leicht ist schwer – Ein paar Grundideen [Humor helps to heal. What is easy is difficult—the basics]. In B. Wild: *Humor in Psychiatrie und Psychotherapie.*

Jäger, W., Grimm, B. (2010^2): *Die Flöte des Unendlichen. Mystische Rezitationstexte aus Ost und West* [The flute of the infinite. Mystical reciting texts from east and west]. Holzkirchen: Wege der Mystik

Lamb, F. B. (1985): *Der Magier vom Amazonas* [Wizard of the upper Amazon]. Reinbek bei Hamburg: Rowohlt.

Marti, L. (2013): *Übrigens, das Leben ist schön* [By the way, life is beautiful]. Freiburg im Breisgau: Kreuz Verlag.

Metzner, M.S. (2013): *Achtsamkeit und Humor. Das Immunsystem des Geistes* [Mindfulness and humor. The immune system of the mind]. Stuttgart: Schattauer.

Repges, W. (1985): *Johannes vom Kreuz – Der Sänger der Liebe* [John of the Cross – the singer of love]. Würzburg: Echter.

Ruch, W. (2012): Humor und Charakter [Humor and character]. In B. Wild: *Humor in Psychiatrie und Psychotherapie. Neurobiologie-Methoden-Praxis*. Stuttgart: Schattauer.

Siegel, D.J. (2012): *Mindsight. Die neue Wissenschaft der persönlichen Transformation* [Mindsight: The new science for personal transformation]. Munich: Goldmann.

Thich Nath Hanh (2016): *Das Herz von Buddhas Lehre* [The heart of Buddha's teaching]. Freiburg: Herder.

CHAPTER SEVEN

COMING HOME TO GOD

JUDITH MILLER

Abstract: Coming home for Judith Miller has meant experiencing God in multiple ways. This chapter discusses how God is the one and only reality, which holds us all. The reality that is God can be accessed in three ways: 1. outside the self, 2. within, and 3. among us all. Conceptualizing God in these three ways comes from a developmental model of consciousness evolution referred to as "The Three Faces of God," first described by Ken Wilber. It is applicable for people from different spiritual traditions, different cultures and different parts of the world. Miller describes the ways she has come home to God throughout her life, and how such encounters have informed her work with Western and Eastern spiritual seekers.

Keywords: *Christ Consciousness, God, Ken Wilber, Oneness, Western Spiritual Path*

Contemplating the ineffable force that I call God has been a core part of my life's journey. Today, I can honestly say that God is the center of my life. It is the place I call home. Coming to terms with this realization, however, has been a gradual, ongoing, not-so-easy, long-term process.

What do I Mean when I Say that I Have Come Home to God?

I believe that God is a loving, positive, immense and mysterious force … that is with me always – in every decision, choice and happening in my life. I am never alone. I also know that when difficulties arise, I can go into quiet contemplation and prayer … asking God for guidance to better understand the subtle and not-so-subtle issues that may be involved in my latest challenge.

While I realize that the resolution of my problems will in part depend on the actions I take and decisions I make, I also understand that, ultimately, I am not in control and the final outcomes are dependent on that inexplicable God force. I will do my best to find solutions but in the end, things will turn out as they are destined to be … whether I understand it all or not.

In my day-to-day life, I am a wife, a mother, a sister, a grandmother and a friend. I am also a psychologist, an author and a university professor who mentors the growth of clients and students. My work takes me from my home in Philadelphia in the USA to Europe and Asia. I support groups of seekers through a psycho-spiritual practice called Transpersonal Breathwork.

The spiritual mentoring work that I do with people necessitates that they expand their consciousness and enter non-ordinary states of consciousness. This latter role is not one I consciously or with intention chose to do. I came from a secular family and my academic background prepared me to work as a mainstream psychotherapist.

But that was not to be. My radical transformation – which very much influenced my work with others – I believe, has come about from no-one less than God.

The Three Faces of God

Ken Wilber, an internationally recognized author and philosopher who specializes in the evolution of consciousness, describes God in ways that fully resonate with me. Wilber (2007) writes that human nature is greatly enriched when God is experienced in all of the following three ways: 1. God as "*Other*," 2. God as the Self, the great "*I AM*," and 3. God as "*All*."

Wilber's framework has helped me conceptualize my own personal journey, and it has also enabled me to better support my clients and students as they travel their respective spiritual paths. In the next section, I share examples of how I have experienced the three faces of God throughout my life. My journey has not been linear. Rather, encounters with each of the faces of God have ultimately come together over a period of many years.

1. GOD AS "Other"

Experiencing God as "Other" began for me as a child. C. G. Jung (1983: 82), foremost spiritual psychologist, wrote: "The unrelated human being lacks wholeness, for he can achieve wholeness only through the soul, and the soul cannot exist without its other side, which is always found in a "You"."

Even so, the idea of God as "Other," beyond the separate self, is a sticking point for many in the West because it is too reminiscent of the authority of organized religion. Yet Ken Wilber, who spent a large part of his life as a Buddhist, now says he has finally come to realize that "a relationship with that *"Other"* in love and devotion and ecstasy … is the only appropriate response if you have any sanity at all."

I believe this is important for people, especially those with Judeo/Christian sacred roots, because in the West, we focus more on the separate "I" as opposed to the collective "We" in the East.

> Without God as Thou … becoming a living, felt dimension of our own direct experience of Spirit," Wilber asks, "I wonder whether it's possible to ever move beyond ego in any kind of authentic way? (Cohen & Wilber, 2006)

I agree with Wilber. It is my relationship to God as *"Other"* that has allowed me to surrender the notion that I am a separate, individual self, and to give up any belief that I am in control.

Prayer

Making contact with God as "Other" comes about for me through prayer. When I was a small girl, I recited a popular children's prayer that was written in the 18th century. I am unsure when I first heard it or even who taught it to me but I would recite it most nights before I went to sleep: "Now I lay me down to sleep, I pray the Lord my soul to keep. If I should die before I wake, I pray the Lord my soul to take" (The New England Primer, 1750, ed., p. 28).

And then I would add: "Please protect Mommy, Daddy and brother Nate" … and, finally, I might also add a personal request … "I'd like to get a good mark on my spelling test … if it's OK with you, please let me get an A. Thank you, I love you. Amen."

The years passed. Mostly, my childhood prayer became a memory. I still prayed to the "Other" – even though my prayers were becoming more "mature." What remained the same, however, was that I followed every prayer with the words, "Thank you, I love you – Amen."

Romantic crises and personal travails as a young adult would inspire me to close my eyes and direct my requests, my anguish, my fears to a transcendent force – far away. Intuitively, I felt I should not ask for personal favors. Instead, I would pray for guidance, for greater clarity and, if necessary … I would ask that my particular sorrow in due course would help me grow. As a child, I visualized God as the benevolent grandfather with a long white beard who always seemed to answer my prayers. As I grew into a young adult, my encounters of God as "Other" regularly brought up questions of whether there really is a "Who," a "Being," out there in charge of our lives?

Instead of an old man, I visualized God as a gigantic smoky gray empty space, with strong and magnificent bursts of light shining through and vibrating with immense power. I would pray to this image … I would thank *It* … I would feel awed by *It*. Sometimes I would call *It* consciousness, other times I would call *It* God … I learned that Buddhism calls *It Luminosity – Emptiness;* I also became aware of the term *Void.*

More years passed. Something was not quite right. When I closed my eyes in prayer, I began to ruminate – who/what was the *It* that heard my words, felt my fears, my heart and my soul? I did not feel known by this great *It*. How could an *It* hear me, see me, feel me, really know me? And how could I feel close to an *It?*

My life was full and interesting. I was completing my training as a psychologist and obtaining a PhD. I had a loving husband and two wonderful children. Life was good. I believed that I was too mature and psychologically sophisticated to imagine a God out there I could not authentically communicate with. And since it was becoming ever clearer to my colleagues and me that such a phenomenon as God did not really exist, what was the point of praying anyway? My prayers were no longer relevant.

Time moved on. My parents got divorced after many years of marriage. The world around me was going through many changes – the Vietnam war, civil rights and feminist movements. A few people I knew died.

What was death? How can we live our lives, become the best we can be … and then one day, unexpectedly, it's all over … we are put in the ground and that's it? I began to feel lost. What was the purpose of life anyway? I was yearning for something more – my warm and secure conception of God had disappeared. While I still sometimes visualized that vast smoky consciousness that had brought me some peace, I was starting to feel empty and alone – I began to search … but search for what?

My Direct Connection with "Other"

Slowly and with reluctance, I had to admit to myself that I missed a personal God I could turn to when I was afraid. That all-important, indescribable support that could be a bridge for me to the other side; that would help me to realize I was still God's child – no matter my age. Help came to me during this challenging time of life, but the nature of the help was hard for me to accept. Growing up as I did, in a secular Jewish family, the last kind of spiritual experience I would have expected did in fact happen to me, in ways that felt shocking. Strong mystical imagery of Jesus burst into my consciousness initially in Breathwork, when I experienced myself on the Cross.

Later on, there were visions of his face, his deep, compassionate eyes. There was the time I could hear his sacred heart beating in my own heart. And then, that startling Friday on an Easter weekend, blood suddenly appeared on the palm of my left hand, in what could be described as stigmata.

Christ Consciousness

Jesus has become the core of my life. He started out as an "Other" – totally outside me, providing spiritual guidance, support and protection. This *"Other"* has transformed over time into a consciousness that fills my mind, my soul and my heart.

In his book *The Starseed Transmissions,* author Ken Carey (1982) shares a vision he had that in many ways parallels my experience. One night, while lying half-asleep in bed, Carey slipped into a state of heightened consciousness that lasted 11 days. He transcribed the messages he received, and wrote the following excerpt:

> Outside of time and space, you are One with the Creator, the All that is, the Source. But when your consciousness moves within the context of a manifest universe, you become the Son (Daughter), the Christ. In essence, you are the relationship between Spirit and Matter, the mediator, the bridge, the means through which the Creator relates to Creation. You are life as it relates to planet earth, eternity as it relates to time, the infinite as it relates to the finite. Though you presently experience yourself as a separate and fragmented species, you are in fact, a single unified being, sharing the consciousness of the Creator. (Carey, 1983: 15)

The Western Spiritual Path is a transformational process that makes a human being another Christos, an awakened child of the Creator. This process can be found in the story of the passion, death and resurrection of Jesus. But unlike much of mainstream Christianity, the mystical branch of Christianity – Gnosticism – teaches that Jesus' story was not merely an external act of salvation but depicts the journey of the individual soul.

Jesus's words "The Kingdom of God is within" is the call for inner transformation. His crucifixion mirrors the surrender of the ego. And His resurrection is a rebirth of the self, transformed, awakened and whole.

The Western Spiritual Path leading to Christ Consciousness has become my sacred journey, and has informed my work with others.

East and West

Tibetan Buddhist teacher Sogyal Rinpoche (Rinpoche & Gaffney, 2012: 289) affirms God as "Other" when he writes:

> It is difficult to relate to the presence of enlightened energies if they have no form or ground for personal communication … personifying them in the form of deities enables the practitioner to recognize them and relate to them.

This is how I now understand Jesus. He is the divine, sacred protector, a spiritual teacher in the West. The Hindu gods and the Buddha, for example, fulfill this role in the East. Yet, as Sogyal Rinpoche says, "In whatever form the deities appear, it is important to recognize that there is definitely *no difference whatever in their fundamental nature"* (Rinpoche & Gaffney, 2012: 289).

In other words, they all point to the same Source, the same God, for every human in every culture around the world. Today, when I close my eyes, I still pray to the transcendent "Other."

I also pray to the Great "I AM" – coming through as Christ Consciousness, a consciousness I believe is growing immensely and becoming stronger and more powerful in the Western soul.

2. God as "I AM"

God as "I AM" is our inner wisdom, the God Self within. It can also be called God Immanent. It is our personal connection with Divine Intelligence, our soul's truth. When we tap into the flow of God energy within, we discover an ever-present Light.

Through this I AM, I have learned to trust myself as I support my clients and students on their respective spiritual paths. In my best moments, the great I AM is what I express in the world and it is what attracts others. It is also where I go when I want to access the parts of my Self that I know I can trust and have never let me down.

Carl Jung (1933) differentiated between the word "self" with a small 's' and "Self" with a capital 'S.' Jung said 'self' refers to our ego individuality – while 'Self' is our connection to the soul – where human nature and God come together.

My God Self in China

I walked to the front of the room to give a lecture. I sat in a chair on the stage. About one hundred young people were in the audience to hear my talk on what it means to travel a spiritual path. Shaoran, my translator, was also sitting in a chair on the stage to my left.

I was in China – how would they react to what I say, I wondered. After all, I looked different, I was older than most of them, I spoke a different language, they did not know me and I certainly did not know them.

I also knew the Chinese people come from a great rich ancient sacred tradition – but because of Communism, all that had been suppressed for over seventy years. And yet – I was invited to facilitate spiritual work with them because their government was beginning to realize that because of China's recent big changes, the Chinese people were feeling a growing unease and, increasingly, seemed to be yearning for something beyond their reach.

I was from a totally different culture … could I be sure that Shaoran – this young Chinese man – would interpret my words correctly and repeat them to the audience in the ways I wanted them heard? So many unknowns … so much to be concerned about. They applauded me when I took my seat on the podium. This was new for me – usually I am not given this kind of reception. I smiled, and began to speak. Shaoran and I seemed to quickly and effortlessly move into a flow together. I would speak several sentences and then leave some time and space for him to translate my words. I looked into the open, bright eyes of the young people in the audience. They were looking to me. More words came from me … Shaoran repeated them. The flow was apparent. I continued to express myself – I spoke of the spiritual force that I refer to as God – maybe they think of the Buddha Self, I suggested, similar to what we in the West call Christ Consciousness. They continued looking intently at me, sometimes nodding in agreement.

Then I became aware that I wanted to know them. Who were these young people gazing at me so intently? I realized that I wanted to hear from them. I asked them to close their eyes for a few moments, breathe deeply and become aware of what feelings and thoughts came up for them. I thought this would facilitate a more in-depth question-and- answer discussion among all of us.

As they settled into their chairs, I saw tears from behind closed eyes slowly coming down cheeks. I also became aware of a very strong energy in the room. Shaoran closed his eyes with the rest of them. After some moments, I gently asked them to open their eyes and express what they were thinking and feeling. Many hands were instantly raised. People in the audience began to ask questions. I answered them. They smiled and nodded with affirmation. Then they began to speak of their own challenges, their own problems. Some spoke of the very strong energy in the room. Others asked what was happening … some felt confused, emotional, perhaps even frightened.

I addressed each of the life problems they brought up. People in the audience also began to address each other and offer suggestions. There was a sharing of similar experiences.

Some had wet eyes – others were smiling and happy, still others expressed pain that was deep in their souls that now seemed to be surfacing, maybe for the first time. Our time together eventually came to an end. What was supposed to be a two-hour lecture turned out to be over four hours. As was Chinese custom, I was asked to leave the room immediately after our time together was over. Once again, as I left, there was applause. I went into an adjoining room to sit by myself – wondering how everyone was feeling.

There was so much emotion expressed, I could not help but wonder what really happened in there. A short time later, Shaoran and a few organizers of the event came into my room, ready to drive me to my hotel. They were all smiles, energized, and reported how people were in a high energy state and very happy.

The next day, I learned that many of the participants at the lecture were in contact with each other, and spent many hours discussing, trying to analyze and reacting to the previous afternoon. What I discovered in the days to follow was that the Chinese people in the last seventy years of Communism have learned to suppress their emotions, to turn away from their very deep and ancient sacred foundation, and to not even be aware that anything was missing. In many ways, they had been disconnected from their souls.

In spite of all this, the people who came to my talk discovered how profound and intense their spiritual nature really is. It may have been covered up for a long while but when they found themselves in a different space, the energy that had been so long subdued exploded in a magnificent way. They suddenly remembered what they had forgotten and their souls once again came alive.

The message I took away from this situation was profound. It became clear to me that none of us in that room that afternoon was alone. There was a divine intelligence that was very active and guiding what occurred. Just as there was a flow of God energy that passed through the words Shaoran and I shared, there was a flow of that same energy passing through me, which I, in turn, communicated to the people in the room that day.

That energy dissolved the differences between East and West, it triggered my inner light, my translator's inner light, and the light of each person in the audience. We were all being led, guided and opened to our true spiritual nature. This was the great I AM, the Christ Consciousness, the God Self within. And we all experienced this – we were in its presence … God was dancing in our souls that day in China. I was home – in this far-away land.[1]

3. God as "All"

God as "*All*" is a holistic perception of the great web of life – the perfection of connection, stretching from dust to Deity. From this "*All*" evolves Oneness, the sense of feeling merged with everything – no inner, no outer, simply, "*All.*"

The contemporary American mystic David Spangler described God as *All:*

> When I was seven years old … the domain of consciousness itself broke through and I had a classical mystical experience of dissolving into an oceanic feeling of Oneness and infinite connectedness. I became pure consciousness, which was limitless and, if I were to give it a quality, infinitely loving. It was a beingness of love. (Gilman, 1993: 55)

Black Elk of the Ogala Sioux Nation (1863-1950) is reported to have told John G. Neihardt (1932/1979) the following:

> The first peace, which is most important, is that which comes within the souls of people when they realize their relationship, their Oneness, with the universe and all its powers, and when they realize that at the center of the universe dwells the Great Spirit, and that this center is really everywhere, it is within each of us.

[1] Zhangzhou, China, August, 2014

The Jewish mystics also spoke of God as *"All"* when they used the term *tikkun.*[2] This term (Frankel, 2005) suggests that we are co-creators with divine energy, which we may manifest through our thoughts and deeds. Thus, we can accomplish *Tikkun Olam* – "repair the world" – by transcending such polarities as good and evil, male and female, spirit and matter, chaos and order – in other words, living in the "*All*" and experiencing the third face of God.

By experiencing God as "*ALL*," we are able to hold the opposites in an effortless synthesis and not be pulled in one direction or another.

My Personal Experience of God as "All"

Several years ago, I experienced such a synthesis. I was sitting in a circle of people at a retreat center in the Black Forest in Germany. It was the last day of a five-day Breathwork retreat and my co-leader, Ingo Jahrsetz, was passing around a wooden baton, inviting each of the twenty participants to share thoughts and feelings about our time together. This was an exercise that we often used for closure, to ensure that the deep inner work experienced at the retreat was fully integrated. The baton came to me as the last member of the circle. Ingo and I sometimes share our feelings with group members because of the deep personal nature of our time together. Those who had spoken earlier had remarked that it was going to be difficult to go back to everyday life, after their intense experiences.

I always have a range of emotions when I am working in Germany – from feeling an unconditional warmth and loving connection with the German participants to my own brand of angst as a Jew about working with the descendants of Nazis. Working out these contradictory splits over the years has led me to very deep parts of myself.

As I began to share what I was feeling, a bolt of strong energy suddenly shot through me. In an instant, I was catapulted to a level of consciousness that felt vastly different from my normal consciousness. Somewhat shocked and feeling vulnerable, I nevertheless began to hesitantly speak out of that consciousness to the group.

"I will not have trouble going back to America," I said. "Because I feel that there is no other place than right here." And right now, here, no opposites or dualities exist – no good or evil, no male or female, no night or day, no past or future, no life or death, no Germans or Jews. The only

---

[2] Rabbi Nathan of Nemerov, Likutey Moharan, p.68 in Frankel (2005)

thing that exists is this moment – and in this eternal moment, everything is possible, everything exists, and we are all connected in God.

This particular way of experiencing God as "*All*" affected me differently from my previous episodes of Oneness and connection. After this experience, my consciousness changed dramatically, with the result that most of the time I feel what I felt that day, wherever I am and whatever I am doing.

No matter what personal or professional challenges I encounter, I am unable to venture too far from knowing that the present moment is all there is, has ever been, and will always be. I find that I hold onto life's travails more lightly, with less discomfort.

Can I honestly say that I am now living this way all the time? All I can really say is that I realize there are always new levels to know and process (Miller, 2015). We cannot be at home with God at all times because our spirits are bounded by our physical bodies. While I know today that I co-exist with God in the multiple ways described in this chapter, I also know very well that Socrates was right when he said, "The more I learn, the more I learn how little I know" (Suri & Suri, 2011).

Challenges and Blessings

I have learned over the years to accept that God is everything – the divine energy outside of me, within me, and connecting me to everyone and everything.

My own particular spiritual journey has led me to Christ Consciousness. I agree with the German mystic Meister Eckhart, who wrote 600 years ago: "Though we are God's sons and daughters, we do not realize it yet" (Fox, 1988: 1).

And the following words of Dutch theosophist J. J. Van der Leeuw (1893-1934) also ring true to me:

> There is nothing in this universe apart from God – God is present at every point of the universe and can be approached and experienced at every such point … and, though the awareness is no doubt infinitely greater than the universe which is its creation, every part and particle of that universe from the tiniest atom to the mightiest planet, is essentially, entirely and thoroughly divine. (1893/1976: 7-8)

Like Ken Wilber, Carl Jung, Meister Eckhart, Van der Leeuw and vast numbers of human beings throughout time, I also acknowledge God's omnipresence. This doesn't mean that all of my life's challenges have disappeared. There are always unknowns, confusions and mistakes to be made.

Nonetheless, I now realize that I always have a home to go to in the most challenging of times. That home is magnificent and immense.

It is Reality itself.

References

Carey, K. (1982). *The starseed transmissions*. San Francisco, CA: Harper, p.15.

Cohen, A. & Wilber, K. (2006). The evolution of enlightenment. The guru and the pandit. Ken Wilber and Andrew Cohen in dialogue. *What is Enlightenment Magazine Online*. Retrieved on April 30, 2017 from http://www.integralesforum.org/

Fox, M. (1988). *The coming of the cosmic Christ*. Meister Eckhardt quote. San Francisco, CA: Harper and Row, p. 1.

Frankel, E. (2005). *Sacred therapy*. Boston, MA: Shambala Press.

Gilman, R. (1993). Between order and chaos. The dynamic realm between individualism and mystical unity. An interview with David Spangler by Context Institute. Retrieved February 27, 2017 from http://www.context.org/iclib/ic34/spangler

Jung, C. G. (1983). *The psychology of transference*. NYC, NY: Routledge, p. 82.

—. (1933). *Modern man in search of a soul*. NYC, NY: Harcourt, Brace, and World.

Miller, J. (2015). *Healing the Western soul: A spiritual homecoming for today's seeker*. St. Paul, Minnesota: Paragon House. Chapter 9.

Neihardt, J. G. (1932/1979). *Black Elk speaks: Being the life story of a holy man of the Ogala Sioux*. NY, Morrow: Lincoln University of Nebraska Press.

Rinpoche, S. and Gaffney, P. (2912). *The Tibetan book of living and dying*. San Francisco, CA: Harper, p.289.

Suri, A. and Suri, R. P. (2011). *Inspiring quotes of Socrates, Plato, and Aristotle*. Kindle Edition.

The New England Primer, 1750, ed., p. 28.

Van der Leeuw, J. J. (1893/1976). The fire of creation. Reprint of the edition published in the Theosophical Press, 1976: 7-8.

Wilber, K. (2007). *Integral spirituality: A startling new role for religion in the modern and postmodern world*. Boston, MA: Shambhala Press.

CHAPTER EIGHT

COLLABORATING WITH GOD

RAINER PERVÖLTZ

Abstract: This chapter focuses on the importance of learning to rely on another "agency" besides your little thinking machine that believes it is the only one that has the competence to tackle the things of life. You can call this agency God or whatever name suits you. For many people, it is important to have a counterpart to whom they can address themselves. The main point is to learn to keep out, to lean back, not to meddle with the flow of life. This does not lead to becoming passive. Rather, collaborating with God implies living more and more in the present in a state of relaxed and concentrated awareness.

Keywords: *dream-maker, mechanical being, leaning back, private and professional relationship with God, the red thread (central)*

I don't know who or what God is, what he looks like or how he works. What I *can* say is that I notice repeatedly how difficult, strenuous and dull my life is when I live without him.

I speak of him in the masculine person. This is, by itself, without any relevance but it makes it easier for me to access him. It certainly has to do with my life-long desire to have an older brother or a more loving father. The fact that Jesus was a man (as was his "father") is of no concern to me. I don't consider myself a Christian even though I feel a deep adoration and affection for Jesus. But even as a child, I found it difficult to address him as God. To form a picture in this sense rather impedes my communication with him.

God has fraternal features for me. I love to collaborate with him and for this, I don't need a picture but an emotional addressee to whom I can relate in the second person. If the rapport with my mother had been different, I could probably also approach God as "she." It is, as I say, of no concern since God is, of course, neither male nor female. But I cannot build a relation to something which is neither one nor the other, which may be due to my narrow-mindedness.

Anyway, I need an addressee, even if I know that the addressee is myself. This is a dodgy sentence because it sounds as if I want to say, I am God. But if everything is permeated by God's intelligence (or better – simply *is*), then this also holds, of course, for myself. And so I turn (also) to myself when I turn to God.

What I am heading for is that the question, who and where God is, does not really interest me. Most religious differences – which sometimes have culminated in wars – seem to result from this question and I can, honestly, not understand what is so thrilling about it. The great mystics have always said that, in the end, you can neither grasp nor describe God. And my own experiences, my former eternal discussions about "the existence of God" led me to the same outcome. Each definition of the Divine turns into a reduction (which can sometimes touch the ridiculous, if you think of the old man with the white beard). The only thing here that is really of deep interest to me is the *experience*.

Therefore, what occupies and fascinates me is the *collaboration* with God. Practically speaking, this concerns the concrete form of relationship: the ways it works and does not work, the inner prerequisites on my side, the disturbances and the daily ramifications. How does it (the relationship) come about? What can I contribute so that it becomes fertile and far-reaching? How can I use it in all areas of my life?

The more I discover how much I like being in the presence of other people (it took me decades to find this out), the more concrete becomes my relationship with God. I find this quite remarkable: apparently, I cannot live separated (nor connected) in a partial mode. Experiencing myself as an outsider in the company of humans *and* feeling connected to God doesn't fit for me.

Neither does the other way around. I can, of course, try to ignore God, but – as I said – this makes my life dull and strenuous most of the time. We are certainly "spiritual beings having a human experience" – the older I get, the more plausible this statement sounds to me. To switch off the spiritual aspect is increasingly like a painful denial of something that is doubtlessly part of me, which accompanies and guides my day, and which constitutes me essentially. This is an awareness I did not recognize for a long time – and which takes me to the question: how does it happen? How does one get a link to God? Or I could also ask: how does one fall in love with him?

In my childhood home, we hardly ever spoke of God or only in a way that mainly turned me off: it was what I, even as a child, experienced as wishy-washy chatter that had absolutely no consequences. I was told, "there is most probably something greater than me which 'reason cannot grasp," etc. (I realize this sounds pretty similar to what I said earlier about the essence of God; the simple difference was that the words, then, were not followed by anything.) In fact, this was much worse than a radical denial, more difficult to digest than if they had completely turned away. It stayed suspended in a spongy ambivalence that invited no emotional implications in either direction let alone in any deeds or action. (Apologetically, I want to add that perhaps even for my parents, the vague remembrance that we *are* spiritual beings lingered as an implicit issue; however, I always saw them as stuck in this passive and inconsequential attitude that neither led you anywhere nor deterred you from anything.)

There is more. I grew up in a block of flats in Neukölln (the, then, "red" district of Berlin), in which accidentally (or oddly) several elderly "believing women" led their faith-based existence (this is what they were called: "believing women"). So, it happened that already as a small boy, I carried around with me this notion of "holy spinsters," as we children called them, who I experienced as repulsive and hypocritical. They always had the Lord Jesus on their sleeve and never stopped rubbing in to us all the wise things he knew and said. At the same time, they were – in my eyes – nothing but irritating old women who, the whole day long, told us to be quiet or found something else to be grumpy about. Of course, they went to church on Sunday and had their regular tea parties with like-minded others. They – strangely enough – coined and influenced my image of God for a long time, and prevented me from even the thought of wanting to enter into a relationship with him.

I shall make a digression now to a seemingly different aspect but this is only a small detour in order to approach the perspective of collaborating with God from another angle. I have often noticed that people make changes more easily in the professional realm than in the private one. Or *first* in the professional then in the private one. In my therapeutic work, I believe that the subject matter is the same in both areas. It's always about *one* theme (I call it the "central") and it appears of course differently in the working space than in a love relationship. But if you look long enough, you will notice that they are variations of the one and the same theme.

Such central themes are, for example, holding back; timidity; stinginess in all forms; not being good enough; the deep belief that you do not have the strength to create your own space; that you don't deserve a good life; that you feel worthless, etc. Every individual lives their personal version of not merging into the stream of life. This is what it is always about. And deliverance is usually a long way off because you have to explore and understand "your version" subtly and down to the last detail before it begins to melt.

As I said, in the professional realm, this is comparatively easier than in your private life. This has to do with closeness. With more closeness, you are more vulnerable and have to put up your fence more effectively.

This is how it went with God and me. I was rather damaged in terms of relating to him, and so I first learned to cooperate professionally. It started with an odd story, many years ago. I was leading a new training group in a rural guesthouse not too far from Freiburg in the southern Black Forest. It was the first seminar of a yearlong group, a Saturday afternoon. I had never experienced such a horrible group. Still today, when I think back, those days seem like a nightmare. Many participants were completely uncooperative, they chatted among themselves while somebody was "working" in the middle and, again and again, someone would go outside because they "just need a cigarette break." At some point in the afternoon, a woman had taken the place in the middle and talked about her childhood family. There weren't too many who really listened, others walked around in the room.

Sometimes, schoolteachers tell me about similar dreams /nightmares where they find themselves in front of a totally disrespectful class and feel entirely helpless. I remember that I had a terribly anchorless sensation in my stomach. I had no doubts that the ship would sink if a miracle did not come down on us soon. It looked like it would be the first and the last seminar of the training program.

I have often pondered about that strange and extremely important day. Something awful like this had never happened to me – never before and never after. Of course, there have been difficult group situations but never had I felt so powerless and beside myself. Perhaps, these kinds of feelings were necessary for what came next.

For the weeks and months before this horrible group, I had been ruminating about an interesting phenomenon. It had to do with the rather improbable possibility of whether someone who works in the "helping professions" could so to speak *collaborate with higher forces*. (This goes, of course, for all human beings in all areas of life, but I was particularly interested with regard to my job.) Again and again, I had gotten into conversations with friends and colleagues about this or had read about it in books or magazines. However, since I did not consider myself a believer, I had never seriously toyed with the idea that this could ever become a concrete reality for me. But in the midst of the horrible group, the whole thing came back to me. I still recall how, suddenly, I got calmer "inside" and leaned back a bit. Something must happen now, I thought, or this group will come to an end today (which – among other things – would have been quite a financial loss to me).

Nobody had taught me to lean back, and I had not explicitly read about it in books (even though it is, of course, the most important thing that mystics teach us about getting in contact with God). It just seemed so self-evident and appropriate and perhaps also the only thing that offered itself: to give in and wholeheartedly lean back. Take myself out of what was happening. Then I said to God (whoever that was): "I'm at a loss. This is the end. If you don't want this to be the end, then you must do something now. So, if you agree, please, take over and continue the session."

At this moment, a horse walked by outside. It briefly stopped in front of the window and glimpsed into the room.

I knew from my previous theoretical pondering with regard to collaborating with higher forces that, if you left it to them, you'd have to leave it entirely. And you'd have to develop, in this moment, an intensely increased awareness of everything that shows up and offers itself. You cannot say "this doesn't fit" or "I don't understand what sense this could make." If you indulge in this kind of thoughts, you miss the moment (because, one minute later, it might be too late). When I ask God to take over, I must not question what he offers. This is not always easy since, as a therapist, I sometimes feel like an important personality and therefore somebody who, in this situation, could easily make a fool of himself.

As I say, this has to become entirely irrelevant. If I leave it to God, I must altogether discontinue to *meddle*.

This I decided and said only, in a very quiet voice, to the woman in the middle (who was talking about something): "Look, there is a horse in front of the window."

I had no idea what would happen next (and was a bit afraid that this might be the final blow for our seminar).

The woman stared for a while at the horse. I got the impression that she could not believe what she was seeing. For an eternity, nothing happened. Then she began to sob in such an abysmal and unrestrained manner that the whole atmosphere in the room abruptly altered and everybody gave their spellbound and undivided attention to her.

For a long time, she could not stop crying. They were the kinds of tears that you simply cannot suppress because there are too many and they have been dammed up for too long. She lay in the middle of the room and cried for at least a quarter of an hour. She could not speak at all. The other participants had come closer and formed a circle around her. Nobody tried to console her; they all knew that something necessary was happening here, and were with her, respectfully and even with a certain affection. Some had tears in their eyes themselves.

I don't remember exactly how it continued. It happened such a long time ago and it does not really matter. What came out was that the woman had spent the first years of her life very happily at her grandfather's horse breeding farm. Then, her grandfather died, and she came into a dreary city and had to stay with horrible people. Her life turned into anguish and misery.

All this she had largely repressed or trivialized (as children often do with traumatic experiences). It had never entered her consciousness what this radical cut had meant for her as a little girl. And how much she had relished the company of her grandfather's horses. She had virtually lived in paradise and then been pushed into hell. Interestingly enough, she said later that, as an adult, she had always had ambivalent feelings about horses.

The group seemed completely transformed. I told them how I had asked God to take over. Obviously, this whole thing was not a far-reaching incident only for the woman. It became a very successful training group.

I began systematically, as soon as the process in an individual session would start to stagnate, to hand it over to God, and I do it up to this day. It seldom has such a dramatic effect as in the story with the horse but the sessions always become very satisfying. All I do is keep me out in order not to disturb what wants to happen. Or, often, I simply invite (both of us) to stop short and not speak for a minute – and, instead, become acutely attentive. It always happens that during or after this moment, one of us comes up with some unexpected news. Or something occurs in the house or the garden.

Whatever it is, I pick it up without any hesitation, and then we see together what wants to develop. Many times, this sort of development is surprising because often neither of us understand, at the start, what we are talking about or why we are doing this. It is obviously important that for a while we don't meddle. And, actually, I think it is enough if *I* stop meddling since I can't expect (at least most of) my clients to have the same awareness or the same stance with regard to the procedure as I do.

I, as therapist, am responsible for the course of the session – and if I abandon this responsibility and leave it to God, something can unfold that goes beyond the personal. You could call it the "field." It is composed (in my comprehension) of three consciousness zones, which seem, at first, separated: the client's, God's and mine. And God represents the unfolding force acting upon the field, if it is not disturbed or interrupted by personal ambition, that is.

By now, I could refer to an infinite number of examples because collaboration has become the rule rather than the emergency solution. I don't know why I still seem to "forget" time and again to leave it to God. I guess my personal ambition does come into play here (even though I am hardly ever aware of it). You can take the term "ambition" in the largest sense of the word in order to play down its dramatic tone. It then translates to "the basic attitude that I (therapist) should be the one here who initiates a fertile perspective." This is what I am paid for, is it not?

If you look at it like this, it becomes comprehensible that, to begin with, there are often two forces opposing each other, which are going to get in each other's way: the field-force wanting to unfold and the therapist's wishful programming. They *must* get in each other's way (from time to time) because the field's intelligence and impact is so much wider and deeper, offering such a larger overview than the comparatively narrow and restricted comprehension of even a good therapist.

All these are assumptions and attempts in order to understand. They are based on numerously repeated experiences. It won't be possible to give proof of these occurrences; all you can do is let yourself be open to them, time and time again. With each self-made experience, trust and confidence will increase. And I don't remember one single situation where God let me down.

If you bring in a lot of your skepticism, the road will probably be correspondingly bumpy. It is a profound (but not widely known) law *that situations in which you engage wholeheartedly and without any concept of solution will always come to a satisfactory close.* (Which does not mean that there aren't situations where we should think about solutions.)

They become difficult only when you try to interfere. A man who has problems with getting an erection would in most cases not have them if he stopped trying to interfere – in other words, if he did not try to find a solution. Erections happen easily if you try not to produce them. The same goes for transpersonal therapy sessions.

In this context, I want to say it again (not too gladly, but it seems necessary): As far as the relationship with God is concerned, there is still a remarkable difference for me between work situations and private matters. When I work as a therapist, somebody comes and pays me for being there for him or her, and it seems appropriate to ask God without any reservation to support the process. However, when it is "only" about me and my needs and interests, it can happen very quickly that old feelings and beliefs sneak in. And when my old feelings come in, the very immediate question also comes in – whether it's really worth it for others to be there for me, to love me and give me the affection and attention I actually would like to have (if I am sincere). Often, I am already not quite sincere in the sense that I don't allow myself to feel that I yearn to be loved. (And how much I have to force myself to write something like this.) And here again, this goes for God and people likewise.

The Sufis say that you don't reach God if you don't look, long and search for him with all the fire of your heart. *My* heart opens when it hears this, agrees passionately and virtually wants only this and nothing else. But one hour later, the whole thing is often forgotten and the gray mechanics have re-conquered the place which had been so alive moments before. And the arguments that go along with this all come down to the point that it would be too dangerous to allow such longings.

Slowly I start to understand that my still existing lack of trust, my skepticism that God would be there for me, has to do – more than anything else – with the difficultly of admitting to myself this deep yearning to be loved. To feel this longing and not know whether it will be answered is probably more painful than the mistrust I put in its place. But I notice with increasing clarity that this old skepticism and mistrust does not really fit anymore. (And I feel warm around my heart by writing this – which confirms how true it is.)

So, for me privately, it needs courage to involve myself with God. How often do I get caught at the same old place in relationships because I don't find the confidence to simply let the situation move along without trying to control it with my usual gimmicks. Again and again, there is this point of fear in all possible life situations which I believe will go under if I don't take things into my hands. And all that happens then is that I/we get into the same old painful mess.

It is this form of simple surrender that I find so difficult, privately. As children, we have, almost all of us, experienced humiliations when we just let ourselves be as we were. These are ancient barriers that are hard to overcome. My pride, my honor and my dignity seem to be at stake.

These are feelings that ultimately seem to guarantee my existence or – if questioned – jeopardize it fiercely. Therefore, if I want to collaborate with God in my very personal world, I have to sacrifice something I've believed for decades helped me to survive in the best way - which is that *I* must do it. (And that my way will work better than any other proposals). I start to comprehend this slowly and not without pain. And I understand (also hesitantly and with a slight reluctance) that what opens the way to God might free my capacity for a deeper intimacy and closeness with people.

To return to the professional area: That's perhaps why in the above-mentioned group situation, my feelings of helplessness and impotence were necessary so that I could start to allow this different level of perception to come into place. Otherwise, I might just have seen a horse passing by.

And it might be important to say that, of course, I saw nothing but a horse. In the majority of cases, there are no peculiar, paranormal signs showing up in my collaboration with God. It's rarely about Jungian synchronicities either, or particular deeply symbolic phenomena. I only looked at the horse with a different attentiveness and a more courageous openness than I would with my "normal" mechanical perception - which would be to immediately place everything in a familiar framework. This is, again, such a crazy paradox: I must learn to take the things I see out of their habitual context so they can reorganize themselves on a much deeper level of coherence.

Of course, I don't have to feel helplessness every time in order to collaborate with God. Quite the contrary, I understand more and more that, actually, as therapist, I never have to feel helpless. But I have to allow myself to *stay out* for a while, which, ironically, means to *engage* unconditionally with what offers itself at the moment and not question it – whether or not I understand it. And perhaps I have to generally learn how to gradually sacrifice my long-established ambition and importance.

How many path-breaking horses might cross our way every day? And if our consciousness is tuned into "normal mechanical perception," we won't notice them and will perhaps lose many precious hints as to how our life wants to take its course.

What are they, these mysterious "fields"? One could audaciously hypothesize that in all places where people come together, a potential field wants to unfold. How far it is able to unfold depends on our willingness to take back our habitual mechanics. We *could* stay out with our fears and our craving for recognition or even "only" our compulsion to instantly pigeonhole everyone and everything. We could, instead, allow much more space for the unknown, the truly new, which cannot be planned. Then, the river would be flowing. Unfortunately, this does not often happen.

It is such a sad thought that with all our meddling, worrying, planning, wanting to be right, having to impress – all these endlessly endless preliminaries – we might continuously stop and suppress what actually wants to come about. This too, is paradoxically tragic.

To emphasize this: It's not about passively receiving life's impact, twiddling your thumbs and waiting. No, it is about *collaborating* with

God: we can learn to watch *what is due to be done* and notice what offers itself as potential unfolding. We have, then, a highly active and, above all, mindful and attentive function. We must engage and really let ourselves into what turns up in front of us - even if it does not immediately suit us.

Perhaps we don't understand, perhaps it does not fit our usual thought-schemes. It makes a big difference whether a client says something obviously misleading in order to deflect from a possibly painful matter or whether he says something "misleading," while there is, at the same time, a strong awareness of the "field" in the room. (By the way, in sessions where I work very much out of this consciousness, clients never say anything "misleading." This could be food for thought, too.)

Once again, perhaps we don't understand immediately where things are heading. But if we meddle with our preplanned concepts, we will obtain results that are only well-known repetitions. Transpersonal therapy is the opposite of any schoolmasterly approach that wants to classify patients into textbooks, into a structure, into a predictable process. Knowledge of so-called pathological patterns and developments are, of course, valuable and indispensable, as is the knowledge of methodical steps. As therapist, I need these skills because they provide the confidence necessary for collaboration with God (or for any good therapeutic work). In other words, such mental furniture must be there so that, at the given moment, I can let go of all accumulated knowledge and engage without any reservation in the potential of the field. In doing so, I enter the mysterious domain of the "beginner's mind."

It is certainly a sensible arrangement that our brain cells are always geared to connect what we perceive with already existing circuits of comprehension. In this way, we won't be overwhelmed by outlandish information. We can better cope with the perceived data because we are tricked into assuming that we know it already.

At the age of 14, I heard, for the first time, Beethoven's 7th Symphony, and I still know exactly how, during the last movement, I lost consciousness for a moment. This music seemed to me so completely outrageous, ecstatically unbearable, and the expression of such a crazily exultant trespass that for some moments, I was simply forced to quit my mind.

Today, it still triggers strong feelings in me, but never like the first time. This is the work of the neurological "familiarizers." No second time is like the first time. And when we have lived for more than a few decades, there are virtually no "first times" anymore. Even if we have never seen an Indian temple before in our life, we dial down the inconceivable to "already existing circuits of comprehension" to an extent where we can cope with it, which means: without being overwhelmed.

This is, as I said, good and appropriate, but in a way, it's also sad. Where children can still take things in without this familiarity-filter, there are comparatively few things that make a mature adult lose his poise. At 14, my "familiarizer" had not quite matured into adulthood yet – rather fortunately, I'd say.

Berthold Brecht tried in his epical theater to partially remove this neurological filter by introducing the effect of "Verfremdung" [alienation]. You can, to a certain degree, exercise this alienation-effect in your daily perception, which can lead to meeting the world with what several influential teachers have called the "beginner's mind." It can lead to the consequence that you are able to perceive people and things in your surroundings with an unusual freshness and a kind of curious astonishment. In extraordinary states of consciousness, this impression goes deeper, goes back to resemble the child's way of perceiving – with a more distinct presence, however. One could say it is a state of increased attentiveness, in which many routine reactions of the habitual perception dissolve. Its place is taken by a wakeful curiosity – in the deepest sense of the word.

This too is certainly one of the reasons why substances like LSD, psilocybin mushrooms or Ayahuasca (or even already marihuana) hold such an attraction for so many people. They modify something in the neurological wiring; they eliminate a customary habitual familiarity of perception and let things and people appear in a not-yet-trained, innovative and strange manner. This allows a much more direct and engaged involvement with what is being perceived.

Arnold Mindell, who has been an influential teacher for me, ascribes to the "dream body" (1981)[1], as he calls it, a similar role of a more direct and engaged perception. There, as I understand it, the whole physical body becomes an organ of perception for "marginalized" aspects of one's essence, in both the inner and the outer world. If you make it possible to distance yourself from your mechanical way of seeing the world, then certain parts of the world might start to "flirt" with you (in his language). You can then, with a little practice, take these objects inside (let's say, a tree) and ask your body to express the internalized object in a spontaneous, fresh and surprising manner through movement. In this "danced" expression, the marginalized aspect of essence might re-emerge.

This is, in principle, not in any way different from collaborating with God. The same pre-conditions are necessary: reason has to sort of lean

[1] Arnold Mindell, 1981, Santa Monica, CA: Sigo Press

back so that the body can express itself in dreaming. The less it interferes, the clearer the essence. And an important part of it is that reason would allow you to be surprised. The dream-dancer welcomes everything, greets the beginning of every physical *tendency* of movement and then goes with it – engages with it and follows it without meddling with his own ideas. As I said, this has to be practiced; learned controls and conceptions about how things may start to unfold are not easy to erase because they always tend to assume that without their help, nothing gets going. This is the same in the collaboration with God.

I would say that I couldn't meet God with my mechanical patterns of thinking. The sixth chakra, the brow-chakra, plays an essential role in the beginner's mind. This chakra is either overloaded with worries, concerns and security-seeking anticipations – and is, thus, imprisoned in the endless repetitions of the mechanical system – or it cancels the mechanics, at least temporarily, and opens itself for a vaster emptiness and silence. This is the consciousness of which Jesus talks when he postulates living like the "lilies in the field." An open sixth chakra makes the face empty ("stupid"), all expression disappears, the roles and mechanical figures, which personality takes on, lose their solid forms. A new basic attitude comes into existence, a trust without reservations. It invites you to simply go ahead, to open yourself wholeheartedly to the situation.

This, of course, isn't as easy as it sounds. A relatively narrow chakra does not open if you *try* to "let go" in your forehead. A mechanical perception does not become "dreamlike" if you let your gaze melt or look at things a bit more foggily. And, as you can certainly tell, the relationship with God does not simply emerge because you want to have it. I must keep my objective in mind, realize again and again what it really is that I am heading for – and, at the same time, let come to the fore the awareness that every true transformation is an alchemical process. An alchemical process is the transformation of a relatively unrefined matter into a more noble one. You cannot only *long for* the more noble one, you have to get familiar with the unrefined one. This is the basic principle of every valuable therapeutic course of action. Someone who is timid and wants to become a daredevil has to take a long look at how he makes himself timid. Only practicing being a daredevil is hardly ever promising – it merely shows itself in a stilted form. The unrefined matter "below" will remain the same.

Nearly every day, I take a walk in the woods near our house. As long as I can remember, how to learn to open and enhance my means of perception has been an essential life-sustaining question for me. And I want to do this to an extent where I can absorb the world in a way that goes extensively beyond the mechanical mode. I often became semi-depressive, because by reading authors like Castaneda or through my own experiments with psychedelic substances, I gained knowledge of pathways that didn't have anything to do with the day-to-day routine way of looking at things. In normal everyday life, I always found myself thrown back to this gray restricted perception. When I compared it to the alternative, it was so dull and so boring that I started to consider not getting up in the morning. With "Arny" Mindell, this need for altered perception came back into consciousness in a completely new way. To face the world in a *dreaming* mode was, at once, immensely appealing and stirred me up time and time again. I started to experiment a lot with my "dream body" and had numerous precious experiences. What was still frustrating was the fact that – for me – they *even then* remained "extraordinary" experiences of consciousness and the "normal" perception still did not essentially change.

As you may understand, I've always struggled with the same matter: that is, how I can step out of the endless repetitions of the mechanical structure of my personality and into a much greater width and depth of perception. What offered itself was to fly to the jungle in Venezuela or into the entirely different culture of India. This was exiting, but did not really bring about alchemical change. I always came and come against the same barrier: as long as the old form of perception persisted, I couldn't help but intensely study this old form itself in order to see "how I did it." In the end, it has, therefore, become more exiting to stay in the Black Forest and study the "unrefined matter" here, on site, for example, in the woods near our house.

Even at the risk of boring you, I want to say again: Everything has to do with perception. As I perceive it so is my world. If my way of perceiving the world is mechanical, then God can scarcely have a place in it. (Unless it is the mechanical God, whom I do not discover in me, but who is put on my plate; the God whom others manufacture and I am forced to put up with.)

So, I go into the woods and practice. Of course, it is an illusion to assume that I can take the world in with an empty mind – *without* the already existing neurological circuits, without concepts. But I can make it empti*er* – by finding out *which concepts I stuff it with.*

Concepts are always expectations. If I expect to perceive something or a person in such and such a way, I determine and control what should happen. One of my first insights in the woods was that by going there, I always expected to have a "beautiful experience." And "beautiful" in connection with "walk in the woods" had to do with an attitude of awe and veneration. I could think feeling-thoughts like "oh, the eternal changeover of becoming and going" or "oh, the majestic tree-tops – like a cathedral." This also made me feel a bit nice. But it did not bring me into actual contact with the forest. In reality, my concepts, which longed for this contact, got in the way.

One day, I stood in the forest and grasped this contortion with an uncanny lucidity. And while I understood, I noticed that I could drop awe and veneration without major difficulty.

Then, something completely different happened. First, it struck me how "messy" everything was. Here and there, tree-stumps, which had been hit by lightning or left over by a storm; towered into the air all over the place; there were dead or still-budding twigs and branches, and then, we got this vast array of brown rotting leave-blankets between black sludge and small swampy puddles. But there were also silvery looming power-giants and several mighty ancient oaks; finally, quite forbidden empires of mysteriously impenetrable pinewood-darkness.

There was so much, all of a sudden, much more than I had discovered with my venerating expectation. It was neither beautiful nor ugly, neither good nor evil; it was all in one. Just as myself. And then, unexpectedly, there was such a different, all-embracing contact and a deep "oh yes, *that's* how it is." It enlivened and warmed my entire body.

I began to understand – as it was for the contact with God – that a non-expectant, receptive attitude fostered both the connection and the exchange between the forest and me. There was simply an open door on my side (which I had opened quite consciously, however) and the more I was ready to be surprised, what happened was more astonishing.

This applies to the contact with God, this applies to work, and this applies to every possible daily situation where I remind myself of this potential openness. It works better and better now and is a matter of daily practice. In the sixth chakra, something is happening. It becomes quieter, and because of the receding pressure, the focal point in the body shifts deeper downwards through the heart. This liberates the breath and takes it down to the belly (where it belongs). When the focus is in the belly, the "soul can open its wings," Eichendorff says, "as if it flew home."[2]

This sounds perhaps like a long continuous and complicated process. It is not. (Even though it is probably a life-long practice). But if the "contact with home," the collaboration with God, has been established satisfactorily and quite a few times, all that is needed is to change into the mode of "beginner's mind," shift the focal point in my body down to the belly and call for the clear awareness to be awake right now and not meddle. What is asked for is a curious, welcoming consciousness ready to perceive what is offered. As for the rest, the flow of life will take charge of it.

[2] Eichendorff's poem "Mondnacht" [Moon night], first published 1837.

CHAPTER NINE

WHAT HAPPENED? WHAT HAPPENED AFTERWARDS

GENNADY BREVDE

Abstract: This very open and personal story consists of two parts. In the first part, *What Happened?*, the author learns that he is to contribute to a book, called *Coming Home*, about God. The author does not want to write, and cannot understand how the image of home correlates with one's perception of God. At a certain point, while he struggles with the task of writing this chapter, the author understands that the "space of life" is the home of God. He sees that discovery as a miracle, and makes an analogy of God as the therapist and he as the client. In the second part of the story, *What Happened Afterwards*, the author discovers that knowing how to live in the home of God and living in that home are two different things. He remembers that many years ago, he lived with God as with a loving father. However, after some time, all that remained of that life were clever words and therapeutic techniques. This is when the author entered a period of despair. By the time the author wrote this chapter, he had already come out of the labyrinth of failures; however, he still was not paying attention to his relationship with God. Then, suddenly, the author went into a "pause in being," in which he was able to do nothing but "just be." Thus, the author comes back from constantly interpreting data about God to being one with God, to where his home is, to being himself, that is, "to aspire to being God" (Sartre, 2000: 570).

Keywords: failures, God, home, life space, therapist

What Happened?

At the end of November, I got an email from Connie, the secretary of our institute. Our teachers' meeting had passed the long-discussed decision that we were to write a book. The book was to be called *Coming Home*, with every teacher contributing a chapter. One of the purposes of the book would be for us to get to know each other better and feel closer to each other. In the book, we should reflect on God, in particular, on God in psychotherapy, and on surrender. The letter also had this sentence: "It is important for each of us to connect to our homelessness when we write this book."

The letter overwhelmed me. The people in the team of the institute are close friends of mine, and they are the people I might call "brethren in spirit." Everything we do together is important and interesting to me. However, I failed to understand this latest initiative. My brain chewed over the words of the email again but they tasted bland and dull.

To theorize about God – why on earth would I do that? All that I do is about Him; moreover, it is all consecrated to Him, my strength and the innermost foundation of my soul. He is, as well, the spirit in my therapeutic work. I am doing all I can to help my clients rediscover their own innermost foundation in Him. That said, I would not want to write many words about what ancient mystics call the unspeakable. All that I do is done out of my allegiance to the spiritual yet "spiritual" is a word I seldom use, and I have not mentioned God more than twice in my training courses. How, then, am I supposed to write of Him? And what has coming home to do with it? How should I look at my life in terms of a homelessness that never was? And what do they mean when they use homelessness as a metaphor? Besides, the word "surrender" evokes some feeling of protest in me.

I decided to talk to Ingo, one of the leaders of the institute. We enjoyed the conversation, since we are always missing each other. He tried to make the idea clear to me, with some success. I wrote down some words and phrases from our conversation: "homelessness = ego death" and "to think about surrender as challenge." However, the idea still seemed totally alien to me. It was with distaste that I thought of the text I had to write, and the obligation to write was the most distasteful part.

When I work with clients, be it with individuals or groups, I often start with asking them how they differentiate the concept of "want to" from "have to." I then structure my work in such a way that it would support people in their move from "having to" to "wanting to."

Alas, in my own life story, I encountered a "have to" situation regarding me having to contribute to the book, and one that addressed the fundamentals of what my life was about. I had still not written anything, and it was only with irritation that I reminded myself from time to time that I would soon need to come up with some text (which I "would have to" write) when something inexplicable happened.

However, before telling you about what happened (and what followed), I shall describe two major aspects of my work. One of them is "strategy" and the other I might call a tool, even though I dislike the use of the word "tool" in a therapeutic context.

The strategy of my psychotherapy is enquiry – comprehension – integration. All the things that disturb us are questions from the great Teacher who is Life.[1] Integrity, happiness and coming into one's own happens when we become able to listen into (and decipher) the deeper meanings of whatever might be happening to us, and find its role in the overall framework of our souls and lives. The answer is there for us to find and comprehend. Comprehension implies feeling into one's thoughts while becoming aware of one's feelings, and allows us to move beyond enquiry into a new vision of what is happening. Thus, we also help move to its proper place the source of anxiety that had operated from the deeper levels of our being and our psyche. In this way, problems can turn into goals to be achieved, and then the achieved goals become our resources. That is my strategy.

My "tool," the one I'm going to speak about now, is called "the light at the beginning of the tunnel." The tunnel is the transition between life and death or between one life and the next. "The light at the beginning" is a transpersonal extrapolation of logo therapy (Frankl, 2000), which opens up a path into a new life of realness and awareness. I suggest to my clients that they recall a shining moment, a timeless one, in which there is an awareness of space folding and unfolding and a sense of meaningfulness of our human existence, a radiant comprehension of oneness with oneself and the universe. I then always ask them: "There, where you are now - where is God in there, as you understand Him?" (one of the contexts when I make a careful reference to Him). And people answer: "He is right here - in what I am in now." We work with what the client "is experiencing," and with his or her actions and life events. Thus, together, we help build the lifelong creative "individual meaning" that the great Viktor Frankl prompted us to "discover." Later, the client and I look at the client's view of the new life (at the exit of the tunnel), which is based on the new meanings and awareness discovered during therapy.

While working on the "light at the beginning of the tunnel," one of my clients shared that it was her "strongest feeling, an unforgettable one, one that emerged when she was coming home from a faraway and alien country." We worked with the "light" and talked about the feeling of

---

[1] C.S. Lewis mentioned that pain was God's mouthpiece (Lewis, 1987, see reference list).

having found her home, and about God, who was there in that feeling. That particular case opened the entrance to my own tunnel. My tunnel was not about moving from the meaningless to the meaningful, since the meaningfulness of what I do is the foundation of my life. My tunnel led me, unexpectedly and miraculously, from the question my institute friends had asked to a new and important understanding of the core of my life, which is my relationship with God.

Now that I have arrived at this understanding, I find it hard to imagine life without it. I cannot believe that, recently, there was a time when I did not even think of it, and moved through life without being aware of the basic fundamentals of my own path.

The backbone of the world as I see it is what I call "lifespace." When I think of what is happening to me, and why, I see it in terms of "space giving me the opportunity," "space showing me the futility," etc. Within this new understanding, I try to experience how lifespace is my home, and not only mine. A home is to share with those we love, and I share my home with Him who is my own Father, loving, wise and exact, and who will never allow me to be unworthy of Him. The home we both live in belongs to Him, and it is up to Him to decide what will happen in that home. Sometimes I act, think and feel – that is, I live with "Father and I are one" in the innermost depths of my heart.

At other times, sadly, it is not at all so. Sometimes I fail to notice Him altogether. Sometimes I feel offense at Him because things in my home break or wear down. Sometimes I turn away from Him, and then I become homeless. And out of my homeless blindness, I fail to notice His overall grand design, which is about creating happiness for me, and His wondrous and miraculous workings that make it come true. The ultimate miracles are His to manifest, whereas I only need to notice them and be joyful. The simpler things are mine to do. Some of them I need to overcome and accept while overcoming, "Yes," and this would actually be true surrender.

So, one of the miracles is what I am writing about here. My father spoke to me through the voices and thoughts of my friends, and asked me a question about one of the major principles of my life, which is my relationship with Him. An understanding of that relationship calls for thinking and feeling, and looking inward to see the truth that shines forth from the innermost reaches of the soul. However, to see, you need to look first. In order to be happy, you build your own happiness. Enquiry – comprehension – integration.

What happened and what moved me to write this was my understanding of my long-term work in the field of psychotherapy, and God was in that psychotherapy. The client was me.

What Happened Afterwards

I had my writing of "What Happened" translated and then emailed it to my institute friends. The text was about what had really happened, and the events themselves and their story were like an American or Indian movie, a tale of hardship and desperation that came to an unexpected and miraculous happy end. As I read what I had written, I was delighted at how all the bad things eventually turned into good things. However, when I thought about the past events and their description, I understood that things might not have ended that well, or might not have ended at all.

My friends had decided to write a book about God, a book for which each one of us would write a chapter, because they were living in the feelings and thoughts they wished to express in the text. Through opening their souls to those important feelings, through giving themselves to those feelings and through understanding and comprehending them, they came closer to God. Through sharing those innermost and sacred feelings, they also came closer to each other.

I remembered Ingo speaking at a conference about a revelation. He had seen how the divine depth is shared between earthly people and the universe. I have also spoken about this at my seminars, and many of the participants could feel that depth, their feelings revealed that depth to them. It seems that our institute members shared an aspiration to come closer to each other through speaking about God. Maybe it was a powerful common intuition: to go into the depth, into the one divine depth, and connect there.

As I was thinking about and feeling this, an unexpected yet very obvious thought came to me. If you and someone else are open to the divine depth, if that depth is the foundation and the innermost core of both your souls, then you are already close to each other. You might be aware of it or not. And if you are aware, you might imagine or not imagine the things you could do together. If you are not consciously aware of that deep closeness, if you do perhaps not even think about it, you might still nevertheless feel it the very second you meet each other, even before you say the very first word, or before you speak out your name.

This unexpected discovery of mine perhaps explains the underlying purpose of our institute. We initially felt close to each other, we started thinking about what we could do together, and then we started to do it. At our meetings, we asked each other and ourselves why we created our institute, and what it gives to us. It turns out that, from the beginning, the institute has been an embodiment of our deep closeness, and the book has been a step towards our awareness of it. The intention to write the book and become closer to each other really gave us the opportunity to learn more about each other and understand, to simply understand, that we are close and have been even before we met.

So, we wrote our chapters and emailed them to each other. The most important thing was that every person in the team had access to what all the others had written, and later, in March, the team came together at a monastery in Switzerland in order to discuss our writings. As the team members shared their impressions and responded to each other's deep thoughts and feelings, the friends – the team members – became even closer to each other or, rather, discovered their closeness for maybe the first time.

I was unable to attend that meeting but I read what they had written, and what came to my mind was Blaise Pascal's (1913: 602) words: "God of Abraham, God of Isaac and God of Jacob, not the God of philosophers and scholars." The God they wrote about, those scholars and philosophers by their lifestyle, was the God of Abraham, the God of Isaac and the God of Jacob. They did not have sophisticated disputes about Him, they lived with Him and interacted with Him, and shared their experiences of that interaction. The book and all the ideas and events it described were for my friends the most important thing there was. That is why they started writing with so much drive and inspiration, why they started discussing and living the experience – it is so very easy and natural to share with your friends the very things that are your life. And because you want so much to share with them.

So, my friends had not asked themselves the questions that tormented me: what should I write? Why should I write it? and Should I write it at all? They had had no doubts or protests. They had written easily and with pleasure about their lives. I had had no life of that kind. For me, *what had happened* had been a problem for which God had helped me to find the answer.

When I use the method, or the instrument, that I call "the light at the beginning of the tunnel" with my clients, that light merely flickers and shines at the beginning of the tunnel and not at the end. To turn that light into a beacon, one has to pass through the tunnel. And sometimes one has to dig the tunnel first. The light that had initially shone through for me, the light of knowing what my home was, who lived in it and how, the understanding who was the master of that home, had been merely a light of thought not the light of the life one lives with the God of Abraham, God of Isaac and God of Jacob. However, that light has ultimately become my beacon.

That happened in the early spring of 2014, when I was coming out of the hardest period of my life. By that time, I had already found an exit out of the nightmarish labyrinth I had been lost in for so many years. The labyrinth had been my attempt to build a great project in which I had hoped to find self-realization.

First, along with a few others, I attempted to organize an institute for depth psychology. My partners and I wrote the programs and ads, but I was unable to see the answer to the main questions, namely, where the participants would come from and who would be responsible for enrolment. We found ourselves in a vacuum, our attempts to implement the project brought no results and did not come to completion. I finally understood that the idea of creating this institute was at a dead end, and left. The project fell apart.

Later, I attempted to promote my Creative Game Atelier trainings. Specialists, including some famous experts, highly appreciated the underlying original concept, which brought together such seemingly opposite types of activity as art and games. In accordance with that concept, which relies, on the one hand, on Homo Ludens and, on the other, on Maslow and humanistic psychology, the creative work, which is in demand, is a game a successful participant plays in order to win her or his own self. A marvelous idea, highly appreciated, but once again, the desired results never came about, and there I was, once again, at a dead end and surrounded by emptiness.

Then came another attempt to create a spontaneous theater, a single-stage space that would have no "fourth wall" between the actors and the audience, and to continue the great work Moreno started and which, later, turned into psychodrama, a theater of catharsis. Moreno (1993) intended spontaneous theater to be a practice of spiritual growth, self-perfection and self-knowledge, a new faith, "the seventh day of creation." The crucial place in that faith belonged to the person, to the one who discovers within her/himself the ability to create and through that becomes akin to God.

Spontaneous theater could have become a new horizon in culture and in the evolution of civilization. Beyond that horizon, art ceases to be a prerogative of the artist and becomes a prerequisite for the consumption of the artistic. For that great project, I intended to use my theatrical knowledge. I read Moreno, studied Artaud and Grotowski, collected material about happenings, wrote scripts and texts, and searched for music for the scheduled plays. My friends and colleagues, therapists and theatergoers, were also enthusiastic about the idea. Of course, the project was not possible without a producer, and we thought we had one; then the producer suddenly said "Sorry, folks, because of all kinds of crises in my personal and collective life, there's nothing I can do at this point."

Then, the final and most crushing dead end was the European Transpersonal Center (ETC). I was inspired by a friend's idea to create a European training center that would be a space for development, learning and international communication and friendship. I took up the idea and began to implement it. I thought that I would at last find myself in that project, in that space on earth. I invited my friends, who were European and international stars of transpersonal practice, to participate in that non-existent project. They believed in me and supported me. I created a program of their seminars. As I was working on creating the ETC (I invested two years of work in the project), I could not imagine what would happen if the project failed, like all the other projects before it. I thought that if the ETC did not happen, I would also cease to exist. And indeed, when the idea of the center eventually failed, I found myself on the brink of physical death. In late March 2011, our major Lithuanian partner explained to me that the idea of the center was unworkable and that I should cease all attempts to implement it. I was driving from Lithuania, where we had planned to build the center, and I did not make home. I lost consciousness and spent the day in the intensive care unit of a rural hospital. The center crashed and I, the former I, and my labyrinth, were buried under the ruins.

Now I know and I feel with every cell of my body and every particle of my soul that what I've been doing for all these years was not creativity; it was inept fussing about creativity. Instead of being interested in the content of my work and how I could do it, I was interested in creating a space in which that work could be done. When from time to time I did seminars, I did not think about how to do them in the best way but about what would happen afterwards, how to get people for future groups, and how to promote my work and myself. While caring about how to implement the project, I stopped caring about what was to be implemented, about the reason I was doing all this. When we were creating the ETC, I even lost the idea of what I was supposed to be doing there as a psychologist, a therapist and an author of training programs. When by chance I opened my own workbooks and synopses of seminars, or scripts of future plays and articles about the theater, I read them as unknown texts, and did not understand what they were about. What I had become was an organizer, and that organizer was a loser.

As I wandered within the labyrinth, I understood the main law of its structure. There is no exit from the labyrinth; there are only turns and dead ends. You can come out only at the place you went in, that's the meaning of Ariadne's thread. And I came back to the entrance. I started doing seminars (I can easily say "started" since I had done almost no work at all during those years). I did not care at all about how I could find people for future groups, how I could promote myself and what I was doing. I was resurrecting myself (remember, the grain falling into the ground dies, it abides alone; but if it dies, it bears much fruit) and getting reborn for creativity and inspiration.

Already before I had crawled into the labyrinth, I had lost Him, and this loss, as I now clearly understand, became one of the main reasons I had to crawl. I was in a deep and confusing illusion, thinking that He is somewhere near to me, and that things are well with us. Since childhood, I have been searching for Him, and at last, in the early 2000s, I found Him, and that was the most important find in my life. However, incredibly, invisibly and inevitably, that happy find ended with me losing Him.

Ever since I was born, I felt sure that this world was centered on an omniscient, omnipotent and omnipresent entity, which can miraculously manage the events of life and be aware of all thoughts and feelings. On the one hand, that entity is always next to you; on the other, it is unknowable and unreachable. I called that entity God, even though none of the notions about God and none of the ways of connecting with God that I knew of suited me.

I enjoyed studying mathematics and physics, and made a lot of progress in these sciences. I knew for sure that the world could be described using the laws of physics. However, none of the religions even tried to explain, using the laws of physics, how He could see and rule all while remaining unknowable and unreachable. I couldn't just believe, I wanted to know, like Jung did. I searched for that knowledge in mystical texts – I had access to the special archives in the library where these texts were hidden from ordinary Soviet people. I read and re-read these texts, I copied them, I admired the experience of those who had seen Him. States were revealed to me in which I could know Him and connect to Him. I wrote texts that were testimony and expression of these states. I read poems and articles by futurists and abstractionists from the early 20th century and admired their thirst for the beyond, their ability to see that beyond and speak about it with such great mastery.

I wrote texts like the futuristic or surrealistic ones, texts that were philosophical and mystical poetry. The editors of underground journals could not understand what the poems were about, but published them and said, "There is definitely something here." It was art, art dedicated to Him and inspired by Him. I felt that He was directing my inspiration. His thoughts and His words were channeled through me and remained on paper after I had written them. I was His hand and His pen. If I had to go away somewhere, I was afraid that the flow of inspiration might stop because He would not find be able to find me.

But He did find me, and the inspiration did not stop. My life was totally devoted to Him and filled with miracles. I went into magic states of bliss, I journeyed in the depths of being and spirit, and I saw and felt what was beyond sight and feeling, and recorded my experiences in words and sketches. Afterwards, I went to the library to read what the famous mystics had written. As it turned out, we had been to the same places, and perceived and described them in the same way. My journeys were not imaginary nor were they self-deception; they were real.

My friends and colleagues who also searched for the beyond told me about the special practices and substances that would help in such journeys. I tried some, but they only spoiled it. The only thing I needed in order to go to the transcendental dimension was my own wish to do so.

I had a girlfriend, who could read thoughts, see the future, and journey into the world of omniscient and omnipotent disembodied beings. She was the mediator in my communication with them, and with Him, and I understood that I was living with Him. I knew what we would be doing and how we would live our life together, He and I. At some point, I felt, clearly and unmistakably, that I do not need to search for a means to connect with Him because you do not need to connect with one with whom you are one, you just need to experience that oneness. He was incomprehensible, mysterious, the beyond; he was one with me and the mainspring of my life, and I was searching for an explanation for that mystery. None of the religions, and none of the mystical practices, including my own, could give me such an explanation. However, I found something that at this point appeared to be such an explanation. It was the "The New Model of the Universe" elaborated by Pyotr Demyanovich Uspensky (1993), a disciple of the great Gurdjieff.

As a young man, I read Einstein's (1965) *Physics and Reality*, in which the great scientist described the basics of the relativity theory, in accordance with which our space is a curved, spherical or ellipsoid three-dimensional surface within a space with a larger number of dimensions. Based on the conclusions of the relativity theory, Uspensky (1993) describes the world. All the objects in our world, including ourselves, are three-dimensional. A four-dimensional being would perceive us as flat figures on a flat surface. A three-dimensional being can see perfectly well the things that happen on the flat surface, and can change them easily and in such a way that the flat ones don't notice.

The same applies to a four-dimensional being that perceives and manages, unseen, everything that goes on in the three-dimensional world. Three-dimensional people live on the surface of a four-dimensional sphere, its inner hyperspace is the world of interconnected souls and spirits, and the center of that spiritual hyperspace is God. I was overwhelmed by this picture of the world, which presented the explanation I was searching for in such a clear and precise manner. The explanation was in perfect accord with the teaching of Plotinus that I loved, with Teilhard de Chardin's concepts of radical evolution (1965) and radical energy, and with the radical notions of Pavel Florensky. The only aspect of this view that made it fiction rather than science was that Einstein's fourth dimension was time not space. However, Uspensky (1993) did not notice that, and neither did I. At a philosophical conference, I presented a paper about the divine four-dimensional world that was described by the laws of physics. The audience included a well-known professor of physics who studied hesychasm, and he asked me when exactly I was expelled from the Physics faculty for academic failure. There was nothing I could say. I understood that I had to thoroughly study quantum physics, the science about the fundamentals of matter, and find the scientific arguments that would prove my notions.

I entered the postgraduate school of the Chair of Philosophy in the military university. Its Chair of Physics was among the strongest in the country, since the university taught future specialists in nuclear weapons. My first education helped me. In my youth, I was so much in love with Einstein that I graduated from the polytechnic institute as an engineer-physicist.

Now at the military university I was replenishing my knowledge of physics, studying to be a philosopher and writing my PhD thesis. The thesis was about the philosophical and methodological issues in quantum physics, and, to be more specific, about knowing objects, processes and structures of matter at their fundamental subatomic level. I stated and proved that the scholar may succeed in that knowing if her/his psyche is ready for future discoveries, if her/his personality is close to wholeness and has reached a high level of psychoemotional development, that of individuation. In other words, in order to understand the world at the deepest fundamental level, one needs to go into the depths of the soul and the spirit. Of course, I was studying in detail the object of that knowing. My thesis was impeccable from the point of view of the physicist. One of the reviewers, a professor and head of the Chair of Physics at the military university, read the text and told me that I had thoroughly analyzed the very complex laws of the fundamental structure of matter and presented the results of that analysis in a very simple language.

In the process of doing that work, I found the explanation that I had been searching for since childhood, and that now corresponded so well to the modern natural science worldview. Of course, it remained outside the dissertation paper. One could say that it was a side product of the dissertation study, even though in reality the dissertation looked more like a side product of that discovery.

This is how it looked, and still does: the universe is a unified quantum object. We perceive its parts as separate objects yet they are interconnected and form an indivisible unified whole. All the matter in the universe, all its particles and fields and empty spaces, are different forms of existence of a unified fundamental object that forms matter and is a unified quantum wave field. David Bohm, one of the founders of quantum physics, wrote that "even though in accordance with the classical notions the Universe can be provisionally divided into parts, that cannot be done, because of the quantum wave field that is an integral medium the qualities of which are one with the qualities of everything inside it, and that all the objects and interaction in the Universe are indivisible transitions within one object" (1965: 202). Henry Stapp (1977: 190-205.) wrote, "Everything we know about nature agrees with the idea that the fundamental processes of nature are beyond space-and-time (incorporating the space-time continuum in its entirety) yet generate the events that can be localized in space-and-time" (1977: 190-205).

The scientific description of the quantum wave field, which is the basis of matter, repeated almost verbatim the testimony of mystics and the experience I had of the basis of the soul, spirit and being that is one and cannot be divided even into subject and object, knows no space or time, and is everywhere and nowhere. Moreover, consciousness is linked to matter through non-local interaction.

That is the conclusion made by the Soviet scientists who had to search for the physiological basis of consciousness and try to prove that thought and consciousness were produced in the brain. However, the studies revealed the opposite: thought cannot be produced in the brain, thought is connected to the brain through non-local interaction. Non-local interaction "happens immediately and applies to the entire world, but does not act through distance, since for the field matter there are no distances and no expanses" (I.Z. Tsekhmistro, 1965: 12-13). That is the interaction, which connects the parts of the quantum wave field, we perceive as individual objects. The basis of thought, consciousness and spirit that is connected through non-local interaction with the basis of matter can only seem to differ from it. In reality, these two bases are one and constitute the universal body of God that with each and every indivisible part thinks both for itself and all of us.

By the time I defended my thesis, all my texts had been published in philosophical and mystical journals. The editors knew quite well what I was writing about, and really appreciated my texts. They were looking forward to getting new revelations from me but I was no longer interested in words, either written or spoken. I stopped writing. I did not want to offer testimony of higher dimensions and states of bliss. I wanted to, and was able to, be a guide who would open the path to these dimensions and states and help others walk that path, which is the most important and meaningful one in our lives and leads to the self.

I took part in the avant-garde theatrical projects that came out of the underground after the perestroika. The companies might have been amateurs from the point of view of organizational status but they were professionals from the point of view of the mastery and scope and depth of their ideas. Some of them later became flagships of theatrical art in Russia and abroad. One did not need a theatrical education to participate in the performances; we studied and learned the intricacies of stage mastery while preparing and rehearsing the plays.

At the time of my postgraduate studies at the military university, I also graduated in psychology and started to do seminars. At first, the program was a short one and consisted of separate segments of working with the personality. Later, it became a comprehensive collection of techniques and exercises for "assembling" a person, integrating the personality and moving towards the wholeness that is about being one with oneself and the world. The assembling could only be done on the basis of the conscious experiences that were connected with understanding one or another part of the soul or being. The theatrical skills that I had learned helped me "generate" the necessary experience in the souls of the participants.

One of the key points of the program was the lecture in which I used simple words to explain the complex aspects of quantum physics and neurophysiology. The lecture presented my concept that God existed as one living whole that comprised all the forms of matter and consciousness in the universe and was multi-dimensional in its thinking. The concept was in complete accord with the modern natural scientific worldview. The lecture helped the audience get rid of the "dissensions between science and religion," which, as Jung wrote, "were based on misunderstanding on both sides." After I explained that misunderstanding, it became clear that the religious notions that my students and clients had agreed with faith in science, which is the basis of the modern worldview.

After the lecture, we did an alchemical practice in the spirit of Jung's psychological alchemy (1997) on the synthesis of the Quinta Essentia. The practice was an experience of a non-dual state of absolute and total completeness of all the being that is and was, and of its absolute supra-voidness. Time and space disappeared, the subject dissolved in the absolute object, and thinking stopped. The Quinta Essentia synthesis "awakened" the deepest and most mystical and transcendent archetype of Unus Mundus, the archetype of a unified whole psychophysical universe, the archetype of God.

My God, the triumph I felt! My notions had moved far away from Uspensky's (1993) naïve four-dimensional model, which now only evoked a sad smile in me. Not only was I able to say, "I do not have to believe, I know," like Jung did, I went further than Jung and was able to say, "I do not have to believe, I know everything about Him." That knowledge embodied itself in wise, deep and refined words.

For a long time, I kept enjoying them in my instructions to my students and clients, and in my work. The knowledge became the experiences and states that were still available to me; I opened these experiences and states up to my students, I invited them on inner journeys and accompanied them on unique magical ascensions.

However, that knowledge had no place in my life as such. Coexistence and unity with the God of Abraham, God of Isaac and God of Jacob, which I had discovered for myself and shared with certain like-minded others, started to feel empty because I placed those experiences of biblical prophets inside the knowledge and skills of a philosopher and a scientist. In doing that, I shut my own self out and went on a journey in the labyrinth.

Now that many years have gone by, I contemplate how easy it is to get lost in life while following a seemingly straight and clear path. When I finally made it out of the labyrinth, I took the path of creativity. Some things I was successful at, and some not. The path, of course, led to Him. However, I did not know that I had to search for and find my God of Abraham, God of Isaac and God of Jacob to get Him back, to get back to Him. I still believed that things were well with us, and, frankly speaking, I didn't think about it too often. Actually, I was living without Him, even though I did not understand it. I did not want to think or write about Him, I felt that words were impossible and superfluous. In reality, though, the words and thoughts about Him were for me a testimony of life, but that life was long gone and almost forgotten. That is why I felt so much protest and aversion at the idea of writing a chapter in a book about Him. However, that aversion had miraculously turned into a light at the beginning of the tunnel, and the tunnel was the one I had to pass through.

I went into that tunnel in spring 2014 and came out in late summer. Now that I recall it, it reminds me of Grof's (1992: 129-138) "third matrix," the birth canal and the death tunnel. The spring of 2014 was the hardest period of my life. On the one hand, I was ready for creativity and I was almost happy; on the other hand, I was practically unable to work because of the circumstances: one of my dearest friends was dying. My wife and I struggled for his life, we did all we could and more, but his death crawled on inexorably, killing him and us. The last months of his life, and his death, which happened at the end of May, were horrible. I still have not recovered from that grief. I am unable to remember and I am not going to write about it. Many of those who read these lines might fail to understand why I feel so strongly about it since that friend was a dog. However, those were my feelings, those and no others, and nothing that other people might say or think can change them.

The Space of Life was aware of what was happening to me and reacted to it. One after the other, my seminars were cancelled. I was exhausted. With my last remaining strength, I completed the semester's program and stopped. It was a stop for recuperation and coming back, a stop before the exit from the tunnel, a Pause in Being.

Pause in Being is a short (about six minutes) yet very important exercise that I offer at my seminars. You can find similar exercises in the works of Jon Kabat-Zinn and Frederick Perls. When you do that exercise, you need to stop all kinds of activity, free yourself from all soul and body tensions and then do nothing at all, not even attempt to stop any kind of activity. When we do nothing and do not have to do anything, it becomes possible for us to just be. Of course, we may be in action and being, yet when we think about being or when we want to experience it, and especially when we want to devote ourselves to it, we need to separate being and action. The same way as we think with thoughts, talk with words and feel with feelings, we can be – to the fullest extent – with Being, the Being about which Hegel (1937: 69) in the "philosophical state of mind" equated to nothing, that is, the being of all that exists.

When we stop and allow ourselves to just be, we can clearly feel and then understand that we are opening up to that Being and, through that, opening up that Being within ourselves. Jean-Paul Sartre (2000: 570) said that being human is to aspire towards being God. The Pause in Being does not create that aspiration; it allows us to find it within ourselves and then to understand that this aspiration towards the Being of God is a natural and necessary one.

My Pause went on for three months. I did nothing, I simply was, recuperating and coming back. I came back to the Love that many years ago I had experienced as a great bidirectional infinity. We know that bidirectionality from childhood: The Gospel says, "Love thy neighbor as thyself."

In my experience and my understanding of love, its bi-directionality was a guarantee of its trueness: if you cannot see what is next to you, how can you see what is further away? If you do not love yourself, your love for anybody (even God) else is merely a thought or an empty word that you utter without understanding its meaning. The object and the subject of that great bidirectional love that I came back to were one, and loving and being loved were one and the same thing. To be loved meant to accept God's love for oneself as a great gift and, at the same time, as a natural and irreplaceable need in life. To be loved also meant to be worthy of that priceless gift, to respect myself and others and to merit that respect. I opened my soul to that Love, and it found its place within. It occupied one of the most important places in my soul and in my life.

I came back to the flow of being. When you are in that flow, you feel that the world is your home. Intuition ceases to be an unobtrusive voice from the depths of your soul and becomes a sixth sense that is always on the alert. Intentions and desires become clear experiences of the future steps in your life, steps that would, of course, be successful.

When I started to live the miraculous life that was devoted to Him, I moved in that flow, I became that flow, and everything that I wished for came true, even the things that I did not dare dream about. This kind of life was and is something to yearn for. One can say that each person wishes to live a life where her/his intentions achieve realization; many people are looking for a recipe or a means to make their dreams come true and are ready to sacrifice a lot to get it. The recipe, however, is simple. If you are whole, one with yourself, the world and God, then your wishes are His wishes and they will always come true. If you turn towards the vain and greedy world, "the one you ask will answer." As I wandered inside the labyrinth, I was asking the world for worldly goods, and the world answered, "What a silly thing, how can you even think that I might agree to make that come true."

I was worrying about worldly things and the Space of Life responded by turning away from me. I heard its dead and empty silence. When I made it out of the labyrinth and followed the path of art, the Space of Life turned towards me, opening up and building a road for me. And that road leads to home. To His home where He and I live together, to our home, where Father and I are one. I returned home, He greeted me warmly and kindly and opened the door for me. Once again, we were together, Father and son.

These lines could have been the last ones in my story. However, I recalled that *What Happened* had also ended happily. And I also recalled that the last but one hexagram in *The I Ching, The Book of Change* (1992:

432) is "already the end" and the last one is "not yet the end." So I decided that there would be no happy end. I did come home, I am one with Him, and my dreams are coming true. However, at any given moment and without understanding what is going on, I may leave our home to journey along a road that would appear straight and right, and that would in reality be a homeless tramp's pathway from nowhere into nowhere, into vanity and oblivion. Yes indeed, I am about to write the last words, and the story will be over. However, as for life itself, with all its discoveries and mistakes, its miracles and woes – it is to be continued…

References

Bohm, D. (1965). Бом Д. *Квантовая теория*. Москва, Наука [*Quantum theory*]. Moscow, Russia: Science Publishers, p. 202.

de Chardin, T. (1965). Тейяр де Шарден П. "*Феномен человека*", Москва, "Прогресс". [*Phenomenon of human being*]. Moscow, Russia: Progress Publishers.

Einstein, A. (1965). Эйнштейн А. *Физика и реальность*. Москва, Наука. [*Physics and reality*]. Moscow, Russia: Science Publishers.

Frankl, V. (2000). Виктор Франкл, *Воля к смыслу*, Москва, Эксмо-Пресс. [*Will to sense*]. Moscow, Russia: Exmo Press.

Grof, S. (1992). Гроф С. "*За пределами мозга*" Москва, Издательство Трансперсонального Института [*Beyond the brain*]. Moscow, Russia: Transpersonal Institute Publishers, pp129-138.

Hegel, (1937) Гегель Г.В.Ф. *Собрание сочинений*, т.5, Москва, Институт Философии Академии Наук СССР [Hegel, *Collected Works*, *V5*]. Moscow, Russia: Institute of Philosophy of USSR Academy of Science, p. 69.

Jung, C. G. (1997). Рефл-бук, Ваклер, [Mysterium Coniuctionis, Red Book]. Moscow, Russia: Vakler Publishers.

I Ching, the Book of Change (Ю.К. Щуцкий. *Китайская классическая Книга Перемен*. Санкт-Петербург, Комплект [Shutsky, Yu. K. *Classical Chinese Book of Change*]. Saint-Petersburg, Russia: Complect Publishers, p. 432.

Lewis, C. S. (1987). К.С. Льюис "*Боль*. [*Problem of pain*]. Chicago, USA: SGS, Russian Edition.

Moreno J, (1993). Морено, Я. *Театр спонтанности*, Красноярск: Фонд ментального здоровья. [*Theatre of spontaneity*]. Krasnoyarsk, Russia: Mental Health Foundation.

Pascal, B. (1913). Pansies sur la religion et sur quelques autres sujets[Thoughts on religion and on some other subjects]. London, UK: J. M. Dent & Sons, Ch 2, p. 602.

Satre, J. P. (2000) Сартр Ж.П. *Бытие и ничто*, Москва, Республика [*Being and nothingness*]. Moscow, Russia: Republic Publishers, p. 570.

Stapp, H. P. (1977). Are Superluminal Connection Necessary? Il Nuovo Cimento, V 40, N1, p 204.

Tsekhmistro, I. Z. (1965). Цехмистро И. З. *Бесконечность материи и ограниченная применимость понятий пространства и времени микромира в ее истолковании*. Харьков, Изд-во Харьковского гос. ун-та [*Unlimitedness of matter and limitedness of application of space and time concepts of microworld in its explanation*]. Charkov, Russia: University Publishers, pp. 12-13.

Uspenksy, P. D. (1993). Успенский П. Д. *Новая модель Вселенной,* Санкт-Петербург, Издательство Чернышова. [The new model of the universe]. Saint-Petersburg, Russia: Chernyshov Publishers.

EPILOGUE

RECOLLECTIONS

JUDITH MILLER

Thank you for reading this book. I believe it is a book that is out- of - the- ordinary. Each time I glance at it on my bookshelf, I contemplate how it came about. This epilogue is my attempt to share my recollections with readers.

A meeting took place several years ago, where nine people sat around a circular table in a room at a community center in Freiburg, Germany. Most of the people there were from Germany: there was Ingo, my colleague and friend with whom I have co-led Breathwork groups for almost twenty years; his close friend Rainer, who has also become my friend; Dietrich; Jaya; Regina and Stefan. These six people – all transpersonal psychotherapists – knew and respected each other's work and, therefore, decided to join forces and come together in a newly formed organization, which they named the *International Institute for Consciousness Exploration and Psychotherapy.*

They also agreed that this institute should be international in scope and incorporate members from different countries whom they thought shared similar values and teaching styles. This is how I came to be there, from the US. Also at the table were Vitor, a psychotherapist from Portugal, and Gennady, from Russia.

The purpose for the day-long meeting was twofold: first, to see if we could agree on goals and a mission statement for the new institute, and second, since we were an international group coming together for the first time, we wanted to get to know each other in deeper, more authentic ways.

How to do this? Each of us a made big effort; we openly expressed thoughts and feelings, we were friendly with each other, empathic in our responses, and, in most ways, were trying our best to be good listeners and nice people.

But something was not quite clicking. Why was it so challenging to bring our communication to a deeper level? There we were, all transpersonal psychotherapists and spiritual teachers with many years of experience working with clients and students. We all facilitated groups where participants go into altered states; we worked with group dynamics, with spiritual practices and in-depth psychological approaches. We acknowledged each other as seasoned transpersonal practitioners who did powerful and meaningful inner work with ourselves and others.

As a result, we held high expectations for our little group, and agreed at this initial meeting that the quality of *IIBP* was going to be dependent on whether we, as the institute's original members, could be authentically ourselves with each other. If we were able to do this, then we believed that our work through the institute would be more effective for students.

In spite of these expectations, this initial goal of coming together was not overly successful. None of us fully understood what exactly was wrong at this gathering.

About six months later, we met again. A few of the institute members outside of Germany, who could not make it, joined the meeting through Skype. Because I was in Germany at the time co-facilitating a workshop with Ingo, I was able to attend.

Again, the same issue came up. How do we become closer and more open with each other – where variables such as nationality, gender, personality style, culture and age differences don't matter?

Then Rainer asked the question – did we all feel "at home" in this group, in our institute?

I contemplated for a moment – and then startled myself by saying *no*. "*To consider that I would really feel at home here is unrealistic*," I replied. *"The Institute is comprised mostly of Germans, you see each other regularly, and I do not. I am also a Jewish American woman – and seeds of mistrust are probably still buried within me because of the German/Jewish history,"* I admitted, suddenly feeling emotional and vulnerable as I spoke.

There was a deafening silence for many moments. My eyes became teary. *"What was I doing here,"* I thought.

Then suddenly, many voices spoke (some confrontive, some remorseful, some sympathetic). I felt exposed. But it was good. I'd been heard. And this led us all to a deeper level of communication than we had before.

We discussed the meaning of "coming home." What did "coming home" really mean for each of us? Someone said that for him, coming home meant being with God. Others in the group agreed. A few were not sure, and thought the term "God" should not be used. An intense discussion followed. We each shared deep feelings about our own very personal journeys home.

The group was slowly coming together. This in-depth exploration seemed like the lynch pin that would enable us to become the institute we had all hoped for.

"*What would it be like if we each wrote what coming home meant for us?*" Ingo asked. Then someone else exclaimed, "*Maybe we should each write our own story about 'coming home' and then put all the chapters together and make a book out of it.*"

A stillness came over the group. No one spoke for what felt like many minutes.

Before our meeting ended that day, a decision was made that we would gather again, for a three-day retreat at a quiet monastery in Switzerland in approximately six months. And during the months before the retreat, we would each write a chapter on what coming home meant for us, send our respective drafts to each other via computer, and then use the days at the monastery to process and discuss our chapters with each other.

This is what we did. The days together were intense, emotional, mystical, challenging … and quite amazing. We finally got to know each other at the monastery at an in-depth level that would have been impossible before. We shared from our souls with each other.

It is uncommon to have a book written by nine authors, unless, of course, it is an edited book with an academic focus. Our book does not fit into such a niche. It is different.

Writing this book as an institute has been a deep process engaged in by nine individuals who bared their souls to each other. One thing we learned at the monastery was that "coming home" is a theme that cannot be discussed at a surface level. It is intense, it is complex and it means different things to different people.

In many ways, the time we spent together felt miraculous at first. There were inexplicable synchronicities. Some of us felt emotional and cried. We heard how coming home for some of our colleagues was often precipitated by major loss and trauma. Recounting and describing each of our respective hero's journey took us to our core selves, to our most vulnerable places. The desired goal of becoming authentic and close as an institute seemed to suddenly happen – on the first day of our retreat – at this very special monastery in the green hills of Switzerland.

But then, at the end of our second day, problems slowly started to surface. We quickly realized the complexity of where we found ourselves. As we began to discuss our chapters with each other in more depth, some of us privately wondered how such a process could possibly result in a published book. We each had different writing styles. We suddenly learned very new information about each other. When "coming home" for one of our colleagues turned out to be radically different from our own experience, there was the immediate tendency to think that the other was wrong, and we were right. Then, upon further contemplation, we could easily switch from our ego-driven interpretation and make ourselves wrong and the other far more admirable.

Soon, the immediate appreciation of being authentic and "deep" with our friends began to change to tension, some conflict and a great deal of confusion. There seemed nowhere to escape in this isolated monastery to avoid what was happening. We were locked together. How were we going to work this out?

For some of our colleagues, coming home had to do with the importance of personal relationships. For others, it solely had to do with their very religious natures. A few had trouble using the term "God." Others of us felt it was necessary to use this term. We learned that for some, coming home was considered in the context of their early childhood development. Others wanted only to focus on the now. The role of being a professional psychotherapist, a spiritual guide or teacher, was implicitly transmitted in some people's writing. Others preferred to share their own private mystical experiences. The significance placed on the individual self versus the collective varied among us. For some, confronting personal shadows was necessary and integral to coming home; others focused mainly on the Light.

The stories you have read in this compilation are very different. They have laid bare our frailties, our core strengths, our inner light and our fears. In sum, we have shown our souls and our humanness. Some of us are better writers than others. Some are rational and write in an academic style – others might ramble a bit. Should we have hired an outside editor, who would have worked to create one writing style and one voice? That was my suggestion. There was disagreement.

I heard from my colleagues: "Let readers feel inspired by our imperfection." It was also suggested that I write in the epilogue that we all realize that this book is an imperfect one. At the same time, we also believe that true spirituality needs courage to be imperfect.

And so … from this perspective, and from all of us, we have shared with you our hearts, minds and souls. *Coming Home* has been our life's work, reflecting our deepest pains and our greatest joys. *Coming Home* has been our motivation for working with clients and students. Our paths have varied, we have made big mistakes along the way and we have also grown through the challenges. Sometimes some of us felt awed – and even overwhelmed – when we glimpsed aspects of what seemed to be a reflection of the great mystery of life.

Writing *Coming Home* has enabled the founding members of our institute to share some precious and meaningful moments together. More teachers have joined us as the years have passed. A few of our original members are no longer with us.

Our journey continues. We also wish you well on yours.

Ingo Jahrsetz, Rainer Pervöltz, Jaya Herbst, Regina Hess, Dietrich Franke, Stefan Dressler, Vitor Rodrigues, Gennady Brevde, Judith Miller

CONTRIBUTORS

Gennady Brevde, PhD, psychologist, transpersonal psychotherapist, professor of PPL/EAP, professional member and former board member of the European Transpersonal Association, member of the Board of the Russian Association of Transpersonal Psychology & Psychotherapy, member of the Coordinating Council of Guild of Psychotherapy & Training, corresponding member of the International Academy of Psychological Sciences and Baltic Pedagogical Academy, and director of the Russian Division of the Institute for Consciousness Exploration and Psychotherapy.

Methods: Breathing techniques, body-oriented psychotherapy, process work, art techniques and theater techniques, processes of active imagination, meditations. Application of myths, theatric sketches and techniques, dance, body expression and bodywork in psychotherapy, human development, achieving integrity.

Stefan Dressler, MD, *1968. Specialist in psychiatry and psychotherapy. After two years of training in neurology and four years of training in psychiatry and psychotherapy (in German university teaching hospitals), he spent four years at an outpatient`s department for psychiatry and psychotherapy in Switzerland. Since 2004, he has worked in his practice in Freiburg (Germany) with integrative, emotion-focused and process-experiential psychotherapy, and has offered workshops in Holotropic Breathwork™ in Munich, Wuerzburg and Freiburg since 2005. He is a consultant and supervisor for several projects (e.g. the network "Clinic of the Future", the Windhorse Project) and a trainer in a training project in China.

Dietrich Franke, MD, MA, is a medical doctor and clinical psychologist who has worked in his own psychotherapeutic practice in Freiburg/Germany since 1980. He is married and has one daughter and one grandson. Dietrich is a certified psychotherapist of the European Transpersonal Association (EUROTAS), a member of the Spiritual Emergence Network (SEN) Germany, a member of the International Institute for Consciousness Exploration and Psychotherapy in Wittnau Germany, and a member of the

Swiss Medical Society for Psycholytic Therapy (SÄPT). He takes care of the monthly joke on the EUROTAS website.
webpage: www.dietrich-franke.de

Jaya Herbst is a healing practitioner, using body psychotherapy and energetic-vegetative treatment approaches. She completed several training courses in spiritual healing and channeling. Private practice since 1982. She is the founder of Energetisch-Vegetative Stressregulation® [energetic-vegetative stress regulation] and the initiator and honorary chairman of the Stress- and Burnout Ambulance. Key areas: Body-centered psychotherapy, transpersonal approaches, spiritual life guidance, stress- and burnout disorders, shadow work, couples therapy. Jaya offers training in body psychotherapeutic healing methods. Supervision with singles and groups.

Publications: Books: *Schon wieder ich, Über den Umgang mit Opfergefühlen* [Again myself, about the dealing with victimhood emotions], Verlag Kösel; and *Evas Rippe – Adams Apfel* [Eve's rib and Adam's apple], Verlag Kösel. Various articles published in different journals.
Email: jaya.herbst@web.de, Webpage: www.evsr-herbst.de

Regina U. Hess, PhD, is a clinical psychologist and body psychotherapist (Germany), and holds a PhD in transpersonal psychology (USA/UK), is a researcher, international speaker and writer, and works with arts and film. Regina is the founder of the *Ase World Forum* for the investigation of ancient transcultural healing modalities and their integration into modern intervention and research. She is faculty at international educational institutes, and is a core member at the Institute for Consciousness Exploration and Psychotherapy. She is a member of the editorial board at the Integral Transpersonal Journal and the forum Qualitative Social Research. Regina is on the board of directors of the European Transpersonal Association and of the International Transpersonal Association, and is co-founder of the Transpersonal Research Network. She co-organizes the annual Transpersonal Research Colloquium. Regina is a member of the Swiss Medical Society for Psycholytic Therapy. Various international publications.
Email: dr.reginahess@gmail.com Webpage: http://www.drreginahess.com

Ingo Benjamin Jahrsetz, PhD. Integrative psychotherapy, systemic family therapy, systemic constellations, psychodrama, Holotropic Breathwork™, private practice. Supervision and seminars in Germany and abroad. Training courses in transpersonal breathwork and psychotherapy. Psychotherapeutic practice in Freiburg/Germany. Initiator and honorary chairman of the Spiritual Emergence Network e.V. (SEN) Germany. Co-Founder and Co-Director of the International Institute for Consciousness Exploration and Psychotherapy e.V. Freiburg/Germany. Former president of the European Transpersonal Association (EUROTAS).

Publications: *Holotropes Atmen – Psychotherapie und Spiritualität* [Holotropic breathwork – psychotherapy and spirituality], Verlag Klett-Cotta. Various articles published in different journals.

Judith Miller, PhD, is a professor of Human Development at Columbia University, USA. She facilitates training programs in Transpersonal Breathwork and Spiritual Guidance in the US, Europe, China and Korea, and has been supporting and guiding individuals on their psycho-spiritual journeys, individually and in groups, for over 25 years. She is a clinical supervisor for graduate psychology students, psychotherapists and counselors. She has published articles on transpersonal psychology and related topics and is the author of *Healing the Western soul: A spiritual homecoming for today's seeker*, (St. Paul, Minnesota, USA: Paragon House 2015), (German translation in Press – Petersberg, Germany: Verlag Via Nova), (Italian translation in Press – Milan, Italy: Integral Transpersonal Institute); and *Direct connection: Transformation of consciousness*, (NYC, NY, USA: Routledge Books, 2000), (German Translation – Die Direkte Verbindung: Transformation des Bewusstseins – Holotropos Publishers, Offenburg, Germany).
drjudithmiller@gmail.com; www.drjudithmiller.com

Rainer Pervoeltz grew up in Berlin. After finishing his studies in German and French literature, he was trained in gestalt- and body therapy, particularly by Jack Lee Rosenberg and Eric Marcus in Los Angeles. Andrew DaPassano became his spiritual teacher. Mantak Chia taught him Taoist energy work, Arnold Mindell the field of the Dream Body. In London, he studied Biodynamic Psychotherapy with Gerda Boyesen, and then became one of her trainers. Later, he founded with friends the Chiron Centre, a place for psychotherapy and training. Back in Germany, he was co-founder and is co-director of the International Institute for the Exploration of Consciousness and Psychotherapy Freiburg. He works as a therapist and trainer.

Publication: *Über die Köstlichkeit der Distanz* [About the deliciousness of distance], Holotropos Publishers, Germany, 2009.

Vitor Rodrigues, PhD, is a former president of EUROTAS. He is a practitioner and a trainer in transpersonal psychotherapy and a writer, having published 12 books from sci-fi to social criticism to self-help manuals. He resorts to regression therapy, hypnosis, guided imagery, psychic defense and other procedures. Currently he is working on his own model for psychotherapy, “Awakening Transpersonal Psychotherapy.”
Email: psicosophos6@gmail.com, webpage:
www.vitorrodriguespsicologo.weebly.com

Tom Steininger, **PhD**, is an authority on cultural evolution and the different spiritual and religious currents that have formed our postmodern world. As a philosopher, practitioner and spiritual mentor, he has immersed himself in the practice of meditation and in exploring the evolution of human consciousness. He is publisher of *evolve-magazin*, the leading German magazine on consciousness and culture. He is the voice of *evolve-radio* and founder of the “*emerge dialogue process*,” an advanced practice in conscious communication.